A BREEZE FROM THE WOODS

LECTOR HOUSE PUBLIC DOMAIN WORKS

This book is a result of an effort made by Lector House towards making a contribution to the preservation and repair of original classic literature. The original text is in the public domain in the United States of America, and possibly other countries depending upon their specific copyright laws.

In an attempt to preserve, improve and recreate the original content, certain conventional norms with regard to typographical mistakes, hyphenations, punctuations and/or other related subject matters, have been corrected upon our consideration. However, few such imperfections might not have been rectified as they were inherited and preserved from the original content to maintain the authenticity and construct, relevant to the work. The work might contain a few prior copyright references as well as page references which have been retained, wherever considered relevant to the part of the construct. We believe that this work holds historical, cultural and/or intellectual importance in the literary works community, therefore despite the oddities, we accounted the work for print as a part of our continuing effort towards preservation of literary work and our contribution towards the development of the society as a whole, driven by our beliefs.

We are grateful to our readers for putting their faith in us and accepting our imperfections with regard to preservation of the historical content. We shall strive hard to meet up to the expectations to improve further to provide an enriching reading experience.

Though, we conduct extensive research in ascertaining the status of copyright before redeveloping a version of the content, in rare cases, a classic work might be incorrectly marked as not-in-copyright. In such cases, if you are the copyright holder, then kindly contact us or write to us, and we shall get back to you with an immediate course of action.

HAPPY READING!

A BREEZE FROM THE WOODS

WILLIAM CHAUNCEY BARTLETT

ISBN: 978-93-5420-911-6

Published: 1883

LECTOR HOUSE LLP
E-MAIL: lectorpublishing@gmail.com

A BREEZE FROM THE WOODS

BY

W. C. BARTLETT

SECOND EDITION.

1883

A BREEZE FROM THE WOODS

WILLIAM CHAUNCEY BARTLETT

ISBN: 978-93-5420-911-6

Published: 1883

LECTOR HOUSE LLP
E-MAIL: lectorpublishing@gmail.com

A BREEZE FROM THE WOODS

BY

W. C. BARTLETT

SECOND EDITION.

1883

TO
A. K. P. HARMON, ESQ.,
THE LIBERAL CITIZEN, GENIAL NEIGHBOR, AND
STEADFAST FRIEND.

NOTE TO THE SECOND EDITION.

The greater number of the papers comprised in this volume were originally contributed to the *Overland Monthly*, and nearly in the order in which they now appear. Two essays, written at later dates, were printed in the *Californian*. The final paper of the series only, has been slightly abridged. It was originally prepared as a platform address, and still retains that distinctive character.

If these pages disclose more of the freedom of outdoor life than the philosophy born of private meditation, it is because the author loves the woods better than the town; the garden better than the low diet and high thinking of any philosopher (who goes above the clouds); and the friendships which have ripened under genial skies, better than all.

The House on the Hill.

January, 1883.

CONTENTS

A BREEZE FROM THE WOODS.

"SHALL we go to the Springs this year?" asked a demure woman as she handed the tea and toast across the table.

Now there are more than five thousand springs in the Coast Range which have never been defiled. It isn't necessary for the preservation of one's mortal system that it should be daily saturated with a strong solution of potash or sulphur. As a pickle, I much prefer a few gallons dipped up from the ocean, or a spring bath from a little mountain stream. Do you think it is evidence of insanity in a hungry man to expect a wholesome dinner in a country hotel kept expressly for city boarders? We will have a vacation nevertheless. If our homes were in Paradise, I think we should need it. One might get tired even of looking at sapphire walls and golden pavements. Did you observe how promptly that artisan dropped his tools when he heard the mid-day warning? Many a man gets more than one significant warning to drop his tools—all his instruments of handicraft and brain work—at midsummer and be off. If he does not heed this protest of nature, there will come a day when the right hand will lose its cunning and the brain its best fibre. It is better to sit down wearily under the shadow of a great rock and take a new baptism from the ooze and drip, than to trudge on as a money-making pilgrim up the bald mountain, because forsooth some men have reached it at mid-day—and found nothing. What we need is not so much to seek something better in the long run than we have found. There may be a sweet, even throb to all the pulsations of domestic life, and no small comfort in gown and slippers, and the unfolding of the damp evening newspaper. But the heaven, of what sort it is, may seem a little fresher by leaving it for a month's airing. It is a point gained to break away from these old conditions and to go forth somewhat from one's self. The lobster breaks his shell and next time takes on a larger one. He is a better lobster for that one habit of his. The trouble with many men is that they never have but one shell, and have never expanded enough to fill that. They do not need a vacation, when the beginning and end of them is vacuity. It is possible that the horizon may shut down too closely about one and be too brazen withal; and that as we go the weary round the cycle of our own thoughts will be finished with every revolution of the earth. There is no great difference after all in a desert of sand and a desert of houses, when both by a law of association suggest eternal sameness and barrenness. There is a wearisome sameness in this human current which is shot through the narrow grooves of the great city. What inspiration does one get from this human concussion? Are there any sparks of divine fire struck off, or struck into a man by it? In all this jostling crowd is there any prophet who knows certainly what his dinner shall be on the morrow? The struggle is mainly one for beef and pudding, with some show of fine raiment, and possibly a clapboard house in which there is no end to stucco. The smallest fraction may yet be used to express the value of that element of civilization which teaches society how much it needs rather than how little will suffice.

Argenti, the banker, fared sumptuously every day. But you notice that he had the gout cruelly. You didn't find him at any fashionable watering-place last summer. His pavilion was under an oak tree, with the padding of a pair of blankets. His meat and drink for six weeks were broiled venison and spring water. What his rifle did not procure and the spring supply, he utterly refused to swallow. He went up the mountain-side with muffled feet and a vexed spirit. He came down *per saltem* singing something about the soul of one Brown, which he said was marching on. It is not necessary that our modern pulpiteers should go back to the diet of locusts and wild honey. But there is comfortable assurance that there is no gout in that fare. And if more of naturalness and fiery earnestness would come of that way of living, it might be worth the trial. There is fullness of meat and drink, and much leanness of soul. It only needs some manifestation of individuality, with an honest simplicity, to suggest a commission of lunacy.

"This," said the divinity who served the toast and tea, "is your vacation philosophy. How much of it are you going to reduce to practice?"

As much as we can crowd into three weeks, or more of rational living. There might be a charm in savage life if it were not for the fearfully white teeth of the wolf and the cannibal. There is nothing in Blot's book which teaches how a missionary should be cooked; and a roast pig, that pleasant adjunct, is only well done by the Fiji Islanders. And so, after some further discussion, oracular and otherwise, it was agreed that precedents should go for nothing; and that the vacation of three weeks should be spent with a rational regard for health, economy and pleasure. Ourselves, including a half-grown boy, would count three, and our neighbors— husband and wife—would make up the convenient number of five. It was agreed, moreover, that we should not enter a hotel, nor accept any private hospitality which included indoor lodging. No journey for the benefit of baggage smashers. No more notable incident will happen on this part of the planet, for some time to come, than the fact that two females, not averse to a fresh ribbon in spring-time, consented to a journey of three weeks without taking along a trunk of the size of a Swiss cottage, or so much as a single bandbox. Railroads, steamboats and stages were to be given over, as things wholly reprobate. There happened to be on the farm of one of the party three half-breed horses, well broken to harness and saddle. These, with a light, covered spring wagon, should suffice for all purposes of locomotion—a single span before the wagon, and the third horse with a saddle, to admit of an occasional change. The half-breed horses, which would not sell in the market for fifty dollars each, are the best in the world for such a campaign. They never stumble, are not frightened at a bit of bad road; under the saddle they will pick their own way, jumping over a log or a small stream with the nimbleness of a deer. A tether on the grass at night keeps them in good trim. Bred in the country, they are the proper equine companions with which to plunge into the forest and to go over unfrequented roads. They have an instinct which is marvelously acute.

They will take the scent of a grizzly in the night sooner than the best trained dog, and are quite as courageous; for both dog and horse will break for camp at the first sniff of one of these monsters. When stage horses start on a tearing run over a mountain road at midnight, look for bear tracks in the morning. It is but fair to say that Bruin does not generally meddle with people who are not of a meddlesome turn of mind. When put upon his mettle, he goes in for a square fight; and as far as my scanty data may be relied upon, he whips in a majority of instances. A Henry rifle, two shot-guns, a small military tent, some heavy blankets, and a good supply of fishing-tackle, with two or three cooking utensils and some small stores, made up the equipment. No wonder-mongering was to be done. It was not in order, therefore, to go to the Big Trees, Yosemite or the Geysers. There are more wonders on a square mile of the Coast Range than most of us know anything about.

No vacation is worth having which does not, abruptly if need be, turn one away from all familiar sights and sounds—all the jarring, creaking and abrasion of city life. The opening vista in the redwood forest, where the path is flecked with tremulous shadows and gleams of sunlight, will lead near enough to Paradise, provided one does not take a book or a newspaper along, and never blasphemes against nature by inquiring the price of stocks. The young lady who undertook to read Byron at the Geysers last summer, was greeted with an angry hiss of steam which made her sitting place very uncomfortable. There was but one snatch of Norma sung during this excursion. Something was said about its being sung "divinely;" but the fact that every gray squirrel barked, and every magpie chattered within the space of forty furlongs, left a lingering doubt about the heavenliness of that particular strain of music. It is useless to mock at nature, for in the end she will make all true souls ashamed. An excursion into the woods calls for some faith in Providence, and some also in rifles and fishing gear; and when dinner depends upon some sort of game which is flying over head, or running in the bushes, one must walk circumspectly withal, and remember to keep the eye of faith wide open. It is of no use to cite the instance of the prophet who was fed by ravens. He had a fit of the blues, and could not have drawn a bead upon a rifle. Besides, if he knew that game was coming to him, what was the use of going after it?

Here and there a pair of doves were flitting about, and now and then a cotton-tail rabbit made an awkward jump from one clump of bushes to another. It was a handsome beginning for the youngster, who sent a stone into the hazel-bush and took bunny on the keen jump as he came out. It was a sign that there would be no famine in the wilderness. Another brace of rabbits and half a dozen wild doves settled the dinner question. Wild game needs to be hung up for a season to mellow; the quail does not improve in this way, but pigeons and wild ducks and venison are vastly better for it. A trout affords an excellent mountain lunch, and the sooner he is eaten after coming out of the water the better. And so of all the best game fish.

Did it ever occur to you that while women may be skillful fishers of men, and will even make them bite at the bare hook, they make the poorest trout fishers in the world? There is an awkward fling of the line, as if the first purpose was to scare every fish out of the water. There is a great doubt if any trout of the old school ever takes a bait thrown in by feminine hands; if indeed he is tempted into taking it, he makes off with it, and that is the last sign of him for that day. That last remark is uttered at some peril, if the most vehement feminine protest means anything serious. Two speckled fellows were taken from a little pool under a bridge, the most unlikely place in the world, according to common observation, and yet chosen by the trout because some sort of food is shaken down through the bridge at every crossing of a vehicle. Two more from a pool above, and there were enough for lunch. There may be sport in taking life thus. But who ever puts the smallest life out in mere wantonness, and for the sport of slaying, without reference to a human want, is a barbarian. These carnivorous teeth show that we are creatures of prey. But conscience ought to be the Lord's game-keeper, and give an unmistakable warning when we have slain enough. Had there been a mission to shed innocent blood for the love of it, a couple of wild cats which were traveling along a narrow trail, with the ugliest faces ever put upon any of the feline tribe, would have come to grief. Their short, stumpy tails and bad countenances came near drawing the fire of one of the pieces. But although wild game is better than tame meat, there is no evidence on record that a wild cat is any better than a tame one. They only needed handsome tails to have been taken for half-grown tigers. If every creature with an unlovely countenance is to be put to death on that account, what would become of some men and women who are not particularly angelic? The pussies are out for their dinner, and so are we. We cannot eat them, and they must not eat us. Each of them may feast on a brace of song-birds before night. But it may be assumed that each of the females who make up the party are competent to make way with a brace of innocent doves for dinner.

If it were not for the fox, the wild-cat and the hawk, the quail is so wonderfully prolific here that it would overrun the country, destroying vineyards and grain fields without limit. I suspect, also, that the great hooded owl drops down from his perch at night, and regales himself on young quails, whose nightly covert he knows as well as any bird in the woods. It is easy enough to find out what the owl eats, but does anybody know who eats the owl? You may criticise him as a singing bird, and he is rather monotonous along in the small hours of the morning. But worse music than that may be heard in-doors, and not half so impressive, withal. There is no harm in noting that the two or three attempts to sing "Sweet Home" by the camp-fire on the first night were failures. At the time when the tears should have started, there was a break and a laugh which echoed far up in the ravine. Nobody had lost a home, but five happy mortals had found one, the roof of which was of emerald, supported by great pillars of redwood, which cast their shadow far out in the wilderness, as the flames shot up from the camp-fire. The game supper was no failure. One only needs to throw overboard two-thirds of the modern appliances of the kitchen, including the cast-iron stove—that diabolical invention of modern times—to insure perfect success in the simple business of cooking a dinner. Do not, good friends, forget the currant jelly, or you may weary of doves and cotton-tails, as the Israelites did of quails and manna. And if you want the elixir of life, make the tea of soft spring water, which you will never find issuing out of any limestone or chalk rock, or where flints much abound.

The little white tent had a weird aspect, as though it might have been a ghost in the forest. It was absurdly intrusive, and harmonized with nothing in the woods or foreground save the white wall of mist that every night trended landward from the ocean, but never touched the shore. After a little time the novelty of the camp wears off, and a blessed peace comes down on weary eyes and souls. There is no use in keeping one eye open because a dry stick cracks now and then, or the night-hawk sputters as he goes by. Daylight comes at four o'clock, and the woods are thronged with animal life. The song-sparrow begins to twitter, finches and linnets hop about; and down in the oaks the robins sing, and the woodpeckers are tapping the dry limbs overhead. The gray squirrel arches his handsome tail and runs along in merry glee; and there is such a wealth and joy of abounding life—such a sweet concord of sounds and brimming over of gladness—that Heaven seems a little nearer for the morning anthem. But a heavenly state is not inconsistent with a reasonable appetite.

Never did trout bite more ravenously than at sunrise that morning. The shadows were on the pools, and the gamey fellows more than once jumped clear out of the water for an early breakfast. In losing theirs, we got our own. In the long run, the losses and gains may be nicely balanced. *Mem.*: It is far better that the trout should be losers at present. The philosophy may be fishy, but it points towards a good humanizing breakfast. And it cannot have escaped notice, that the greater part of that philosophy which the world is in no hurry to crucify points towards the dinner-table.

Did it ever strike you that the asceticism of the middle ages, which retreated to the cloister content with water-cresses as a bill of fare, was never very fruitful of high and profound discourse? The philosopher who goes up into the clouds to talk, and prefers gruel to trout before going, makes an epigastric mistake. He has taken in the wrong ballast; and has omitted some good phosphorescent material, which might have created a nimbus around his head as he entered the clouds. A mistake in the gastric region leads to errors of the head and heart. I do not know whether there is any ground of hope for a people who have not only invented cast-iron stoves, but have invented "help" in the form of the she-Titans who have made a wholesome dinner well-nigh impossible. Death on a pale horse is poetical enough. But death in the black stove of many a kitchen is terribly realistic. If these trout were to be cooked by "hireling hands," the very woods would be desecrated, and the smoke of the sacrifice would be an abomination.

Does a brook trout ever become a salmon trout? But the former goes down to the sea, and comes back the next year a larger fish. He ascends the same stream, and may be a foot or more in length, according to the size of the stream. I refer, of course, to those Coast Range streams which communicate with the ocean. If a bar or lagoon is formed at the mouth of a stream, so that it is closed for a few months, and nearly all the fish are taken out by the hook, on the opening of the lagoon or creek a fresh supply of trout will come in from the ocean, differing in no conceivable way from brook trout, except that they are larger. They take the grasshopper and the worm like honest fish bred up to a country diet. Some ichthyologist may show a distinction without a difference. The camp-fire reveals none.

The ocean slope of the Coast Range is much the best for a summer excursion. The woods and the waters are full of life. There is a stretch of sixty miles or more from the San Gregorio Creek in San Mateo County, to the Aptos Creek on Monterey Bay, in Santa Cruz County, where there is an average of one good trout stream for every five miles of coast line. There are wooded slopes, dense redwood forests, and mountains in the background where the lion still has a weakness for sucking colts, and the grizzly will sometimes make a breakfast on a cow, in default of tender pigs. But neither lion nor bear is lord of the forest. Both are sneaking cowards, the lion not even fighting for her whelps. It is better, however, on meeting either, not to prolong the scrutiny, until you have surveyed a tree every way suitable for climbing. The "shinning" having been done, you can make up faces and fling back defiance with some show of coolness. Then all along there is a fore-ground of yellow harvest fields, farm-houses and orchards; the cattle cluster under the evergreen oaks at mid-day. Wide off is the great sounding sea with its fretting shore line and its eternal reach of waters—so near and yet so remote. Low down on the horizon are the white specks of ships drawing near from the other side of the globe—coming perhaps from the dear old home to lay treasures at your feet in the new one—linking the new and the old together by this swift and silent journey, begun as of yesterday, and ended to-day. There is no place afar off. The palms lift up their "fronded" heads just over there; and the cocoanut drops down as from an opening heaven—more is the shame that those frowsy, low-browed cannibals are not content therewith, but so affect the rib roast of a white man, and that too in a tropical climate! If men would always look up for their food they might become angels. But looking down, they may yet become tadpoles or demons. It needs but a little Buddhism grafted on to the development theory to turn some of the human species back into devil-fish. For when one is wholly given up to seek his prey by virtue of suction and tentacula, he might as well live under water as out of it. It might be hard to go back and begin as a crocodile; but if some of our species have once been there and show no improvement worthy of mention since, why the sooner these voracious, jaw-snapping creatures are turned back perhaps the better. Ketchum has made a hundred thousand dollars this year in buying up doubtful titles and turning widows and orphans out of their homes. Tell me, oh Brahmin, if this man was not a crocodile a thousand years ago? And if he slips any where a link in his chain of development, where will he be a thousand years hence?

It is a good thing to pitch the tent hard by the seashore once in a while. Salt is preservative; and there is a tonic in the smell of sea weed. Your best preserved men and women have been duly salted. The deer sometimes come down to get a sip of saline water, and are partial to mineral springs, which one can find every few miles along the mountain slopes. The sea weeds, or mosses, are in their glory. Such hues of carnation and purple, and such delicate tracery as you shall never see in any royal garden. A hook was thrown in for the fish, perchance, with the dyes of Tyrian purple. But there came out a great wide-mouthed, slimy eel, which was kicked down the beach into the water, with a hint never to reveal so much ugliness again on any shore of the round world. Your sea-lion has no beauty to speak of; but he is an expert fisher and knows how to dry himself upon the rocks. When a hundred of them take to the water, with their black heads bobbing about, they might be taken for so many shipwrecked contrabands. How many ages were required for the ocean to quarry these grains of sand, which under a glass, become cubes and pentagons as goodly as the stones of Venice? No more under this head, for "quahaugs" and mussels are terribly anti-suggestive.

The young quails are only half-grown; but they run about in very wantonness in all directions. How keen is the instinct of danger in every tenant of the woods; and yet birds hop about in all directions with a consciousness that no evil will befall them. A couple of wood-peckers on a trunk of a tree just overhead, have curiously ribbed and beaded it up with acorns fitted into holes for winter use. So nicely is the work done, and so exact the fit, that the squirrels cannot get them out. And yet the wild doves which we want for our breakfast, flit away upon the first sign of approach. The era of shot-guns is not a millennium era, and the screech of a bursting shell is not exactly a psalm of life. The tenderness of the Hindoo in the matter of taking life, for food, I suspect, is because of his philosophy. Soul transmigration holds him in check, otherwise he might be found eating his grand-mother. But a school-girl riots on tender lambs, and is not a whit afraid of eating her ancestors. There is a curious linking of innocence with blood-shedding in our times, enough to suggest an unconscious cannibalism, one remove from that of the happy islanders.

An old farmer came up to see us, attracted by the white tent, and having a lurking suspicion that we might be squatters. He confirmed the theory that the flow of water from springs in this region was permanently increased by the great earthquake. "You see," said he, "it gave natur' a powerful jog." After the shock, a column of dust arose from the chalk cliffs and falling banks on the shore line, which could have been seen for twenty miles. There was a noise as of the rumbling of chariots in the mountain tops, and the smoke went up as from the shock of armies in battle. The great sea was silent for a moment, and then broke along the shore with a deep sigh as though some mighty relief had come at last. All the trees of the mountain sides bowed their heads, as if adoring that Omnipotence which made the mountains tremble at its touch. If one could have been just here, he might have seen the grandest sight of ages; for this was the very focus of the earthquake. As it was, we got no impression of that event above a suspicion that a mad bull was butting away at the northwest corner of a little country church, with some alarming signs that he was getting the best of the encounter.

One learns to distinguish the sounds of this multitudinous life in the woods, after a few days, with great facility. The bark of the coyote becomes as familiar as that of a house dog. But there is the solitary chirp of a bird at midnight, never heard after daylight, of which beyond this we know nothing. We know better from whence come the cries, as of a lost child at night, far up the mountain. The magpies and the jays hop round the tent for crumbs; and a coon helped himself from the sugar box one day in our absence. He was welcome, though a question more nice than wise was raised as to whether, on that occasion, his hands and nose were clean. There is danger of knowing too much. It is better not to know a multitude of small things which are like nettles to the soul. What strangely morbid people are those who can suggest more unpleasant things in half an hour than one ought to hear in a life-time! Did I care before the question was raised, whether the coon's nose were clean or otherwise? Now there is a lurking suspicion that it was not. If you offer your friend wine, is it necessary to tell him that barefooted peasants trampled out the grapes? Is honeycomb any the sweeter for a confession that a bee was also ground to pulp between the teeth? We covet retentive memories. But more trash is laid up than most people know what to do with. There is great peace and blessedness in the art of forgetfulness. The memory of one sweet, patient soul is better than a record of a thousand selfish lives.

It was a fine conceit, and womanly withal, which wove a basket out of plantain rods and clover, and brought it into camp filled with wild strawberries. Thanks, too, that the faintest tints of carnation are beginning to touch cheeks that were so pallid a fortnight ago. Every spring bursting from the hill-side is a fountain of youth, although none have yet smoothed out certain crow tracks. The madrono, the most brilliant of the forest trees, sheds its outer bark every season; when the outer rind curls up and falls off, the renewed tree has a shaft polished like jasper or emerald. When humanity begins to wilt, what a pity that the cuticle does not peel as a sign of rejuvenation! There is also a hint of a sanitary law requiring people averse to bathing to peel every spring.

There is a sense of relief in getting lost now and then in the impenetrable fastnesses of the woods; and a shade of novelty in the thought that no foot-fall has been heard in some of these dells and jungles for a thousand years. It is not so easy a matter to get lost after all. The bark of every forest tree will show which is the north side, and a bright cambric needle dropped gently upon a dipper of water is a compass of unerring accuracy. A scrap of old newspaper serves as a connecting link with the world beyond. The pyramids were probably the first newspapers—a clumsy but rather permanent edition. Stereotyping in granite was the pioneer process. Then came the pictured rocks—the illustrated newspaper of the aborigines, free, so far as I know, from the diabolism which pollutes the pictorial papers of our time. There are some heights of civilization which are the fruitful subject of gabble and mild contemplation. But who fathoms the slums so deep and bottomless, out of whose depths springs the inspiration of some of the illustrated prints of our time? Photography is the herald of pictorial illustrations which are yet to flood the world. The mentotype has not yet been discovered—a little machine to take the impression of the secret thoughts of a friend, as now his features are transfixed in the twinkling of an eye. The world is not yet sober and circumspect enough for this last invention. And these interior lives might lose something of imaginary symmetry by turning inside out.

But let us hope that the musician is born who will yet come to the woods and take down all the bird songs. What a splendid baritone the horned owl has! Who has written the music of the orioles and thrushes? Who goes to these bird operas at four o'clock in the morning? There is room for one fresh, original music book, the whole of which can be written at a few sittings upon a log just where the forests are shaded off into copses and islands of verdure beyond.

It is something to have lived three weeks without a sight of the sheriff, the doctor or the undertaker. Something of a victory to have passed out from under the burden of intense anxiety into a condition of serene indifference as to how this boisterous old world was getting on. If so much as a fugitive letter had reached us, it would have been construed into a mild case of assault and battery. The business of rejuvenation commences with lying down on the ground at night with the head due north, that the polar current may strike the weary brain first and gently charge the whole mortal system. The days of renewal may end by circumventing a two-pound trout, or with a long range rifle shooting at a running deer. But as no pilgrim ever reached the gates of Paradise with a pack on his back, so it is reasonably certain that heaven never came down to one who carried his burden into the wilderness in vacation.

What a great repose there is in these mountains draped in purple and camping like giants hard by the sea! And yet what an infinite shifting of light and shadow there is on sea and shore! Is the artist yet to be born on this soil who will paint the mountains in the glory of an evening transfiguration; or who will catch the inspiration of these grand defiles, opening vistas, and landscapes ripened and subdued under the harvest sun? We will leave him our bill of fare, that he may take heart on finding that while fame follows translation, a good dinner may safely precede that event. And as for you, oh friend, with the sallow face and sunken eyes—you had better get to the woods and read it for very life.

LOCUSTS AND WILD HONEY.[1]

It matters little how one betakes himself to the wilderness, so that he gets there in some fitting mood to enjoy its great hospitality. If a bruised and battered guest, so much the more need of the profound peace and restfulness of the woods. There is a fine contrast in the autumn tints of yellow stubble fields set with the unfading green of oaks, like emeralds in settings of gold. The mysteries of the uplifted mountains are veiled in with a dreamy haze, as if all harsh and jerky outlines were the unfinished places yet to be rounded into fullness and beauty before the day of unveiling comes. These mighty throes of nature may be in accordance with some law of adjustment working towards an eternal perfection of finish, of which we have not yet attained so much as a dim conception. If our playhouses are toppled over, so much the better for some of the shams which now and then need the wholesome revision of fires and earthquakes. You see that ambitious wooden palace down the valley. What does it symbolize more than pretence, weakness and barrenness of all æsthetic culture? Some day nature will feel the affront, and this blot in the foreground of a noble picture will be gone. Is it because this type of civilization is but for a day, that the habitations of men are built for a day also? Where do our architects get their inspiration, that they cut such fantastic capers in wood? It might be well to put a new padlock on the tomb of Cicero before any further imitations of the villa at Tusculum are perpetrated. The savage leaves behind some show of broken pottery, or at least, here and there, an arrowhead of flint. We do not build well enough to secure any respectable ruins. What other antiquities, besides debts, are we likely to bequeath to posterity?

The trailing dust of the beaten thoroughfare comes to an end at last. The ox-teams have crawled down into the valley, more patient than the driver, who causes a perpetual series of undulations to run along their backs by an inhuman prodding. There are some vocations which seem to develop all the hatefulness and cruelty of human nature, and this is evidently one of them. In five minutes more there will be no visible sign of civilization in all the horizon. If one is piqued at the silence of a reception in the wilderness, let him consider how gracious it is, withal. It will grow upon him from day to day, until he may come to think that these very solitudes have been waiting for his coming a thousand years. It is not to go apart from ourselves, but to recover a more intense self-consciousness, that we need this seclusion. The ceaseless jar and uproar of life set in a hard materialism at last, because there has been an absence of all softening influences and all seasons

---

[1] As the title of this paper was adopted more than *eleven* years ago, it has not been deemed expedient to change it because Mr. John Burroughs has recently chosen it as the title of his book.

of communion. It is a small thing that the dead are sometimes turned to stone by some chemistry of nature. But what of the living who are every day turning to stone by an increasing deadness to all human sympathies?

The host is at home in the wilderness, but you may not see his face for many a day. In the meantime there is the guest chamber; enter and make no ado about it. The trees overarch you gently, and bend with graceful salutations; the rocks are most generous hearth-stones, and the pools under the cliffs are large enough for a morning splash. You have only to climb the precipice yonder to count more towns and villages than you have fingers. But the sight is not worth the effort, since one needs to pray earnestly for deliverance from both. If most country villages on this coast are not so many blots upon otherwise fine landscapes, how much do they fall short of them? The authorities of the most favored town in the State, so far as climate and physical characteristics go, could think of nothing better than to destroy a line of Mission willows, extending through the main street for nearly a mile—every tree a monument of historic interest—and then, with innocent boorishness, looked up to the faces of men who were ashamed of them, for some token of approval. Tree-murder has culminated, let us hope, since Time has been busy swinging his scythe close upon the heels of the culprits. There may be hope for the next generation. The children born upon the soil may get a better inspiration, and draw a more generous life from the earth which nourishes them. How, otherwise, shall these dreary highways and barren villages be translated from ugliness to beauty? What a divine challenge do these encompassing mountains and grandest of forests send out to men to cease defiling the earth!

It is not so much a question whether the "coming man" will be a wine-bibber, as whether the wilderness and the solitary place shall be glad for him. Will he plant trees? Will he train rivulets adown the mountains into stone fountains by dusty roadsides? Will he refuse to cut down trees because they are old, with as sturdy a decision as he would refrain from cutting a man's legs off because he chanced to be old and venerable? Will he recognize the great truth that the earth is the garden of the Lord, and that he is sent forth to dress it, and make it, if possible, still more beautiful? If he will not, by all that is good, let a message be sent to the "coming man" not to come.

What a large freedom there is in the wilderness! You come and go with a consciousness that you will be fed and lodged in a manner both befitting you and your host. There are no pressing attentions, and no snobbery to offend. Mr. Bullion said at his feast that he had made more than a quarter of a million of dollars by some lucky ventures this year; and that he is interested in several horses of a remarkably fast gait. Did he propose to make some grateful return for so much good fortune? Would he found a library? endow a school? encourage some scientific expedition? become a generous patron of the struggling literature of the new commonwealth? He had thought of none of these things. Nor did it occur to him how much emptiness there was at the feast. It is saddest of all that so many of our rich men neither recognize times nor opportunities. They have not yet learned to make a feast an occasion of noble deeds. Of grosser hospitality there is no lack; but the lame, the halt, and the blind, are none the better for it.

There is something ignoble in reducing the problem of life to a mere game of "keeps." The world is probably mortgaged or put in pawn for more than it is worth, considering how much rubbish goes with it. The wrappers of Egyptian mummies of high lineage, which were wound up four thousand years ago, have been sold in our times for paper-stock. But will the men of these times, who boast that they have got the world in pawn, contribute so much as one nether garment to posterity four thousand years hence? The world changes hands every thirty years, and a new set of pawn-keepers appears; but it is the same old grip. There will be confusion yet, when the secret is found out that the world is worth only a moiety of the sum for which it is pledged, and there is a general call for collaterals.

It is not safe to despise this tonic of the wilderness. Most men do not know how small they are until they go forth into some larger place. It is good to have illusions dispelled in a healthy way. A man is great in the counting-room, pulpit or forum, because no one has thought it worth the while to dispute the assumption. The position held at first by sufferance may ripen into a possessory title, provided he sticks to his claim.

The *pholas* wears a round hole by much scouring and attrition in the rock, and is stronger and greater in that hole than any other occupant can be. The "sphere is filled," and what more would you have? There is an excess of little great men, who have managed by much grinding and abrasion to wear a hole in the rock, into which they fit with surprising accuracy. They are great within their own dominion; but how small the moment they are pushed beyond it! No violence can be too harsh which breaks off the petty limitations of one's life. The valley through which men are called to walk ought to widen every day, until some grand outlook is gained. It is not the gentle south-wind, but the blast of the hurricane, which makes them move on. And when one is violently wrenched out of his place, let him accept it as a Divine interposition to save him from eternal littleness.

There is that spring yonder under the shelving rock, having a trace of sulphur and iron, and possibly, some other qualities for physical regeneration. For two hours at mid-day there has been a succession of birds and beasts to its waters. Curiously enough, there has been no collision; but every kind in its own order. The roe, with a half-grown fawn, comes down early in the morning; and as the heat of mid-day increases, coveys of quails, led by the parent-birds, emerge from the thickets, and trail along to the spring. Later still, orioles, thrushes, robins, linnets, and a wild mockingbird without any name, go down not only to drink, but to lave in the waters. You may watch for days and months, but you will never see the hawk or the crow, or any unclean bird do this thing. But birds of song, which have neither hooked beaks nor talons, sprinkle themselves with purifying waters, and are innocent of all violence and blood. The spring is not only a tonic, but it serves to take the conceit out of a ponderous man who has been putting on the airs of Wisdom in the woods. He, too, went down on "all-fours" to drink; and such an ungraceful figure did this counting-house prince make, and blew so like a hippopotamus backing out of the ooze and mire, that all the woods rang with wildest mirth. But a lad, bending the visor of his cap, lifted the water to his mouth, and drank erect like one to the manor born. For the space of half an hour the great man was as humble as a child, and there was no more wisdom in him. But the spirit of divination overtook him at last; with a tape line he set about measuring the girth of the noblest redwood tree of the forest; and with pencil in hand was calculating the number of thousand feet of inch-boards it would make, if cut up at the mills! If the gentle hamadryad which, for aught I know, still dwelleth in every living tree, saw this gross affront, there were utterances which were nigh unto cursing. Were the forests made for no better ends than this sordid wood-craft which hews down and saws them into deals for dry-good boxes and the counters of shop-keepers? There is not one tree too many on this round globe; and the whole herd of wood craftsmen ought to be served with notices to set out a new tree for every one destroyed, or quit at once.

It is worth the inquiry, at what point that tendency in modern civilization is to be arrested, which is hastening the world on to barrenness and desolation. The sites of ruined cities are deserts often; but rarely is one overgrown with forest trees; as though nature were still in revolt, and had no heart for renewal, where for ages she has been ravaged and impoverished by multitudinous populations. Observe, too, how nature shifts her burdens. The sand drifts to-day over the foundations of the vastest cities of antiquity. But when the great cycle of rest is filled out, if so be that the old verdure is restored, what wastes may there not be, and what drifting sands over buried cities in the heart of this continent? What ravages, too, are these new demons yet to commit upon the forests, as they go up and down the mountain sides with wheels of thunder and eyes of flame? Are all the trees of the woods to be offered up to these new idols of civilization?

All sounds are musical in the woods, and the far-off tinkling of a cow-bell is wondrously grateful to the ear. There is nothing marvelous in the sharpened senses of an Indian. This half-grown lad is already a match for the best of them. There is not a sound in the woods, however obscure, that he does not rightly interpret; and I have more than once been misled by his counterfeit imitations of game birds and wild animals. No Indian can reason from observation so accurately as he whose intellect has had the schooling of nature grafted upon the discipline of books. The sharpest insight into nature is never given to the savage, but to him whose grosser senses have been purged, and whose vision is clarified by some wisdom which is let down from above.

All healthy souls love the society of trees; and the mold which feeds them is a better fertilizer of thought than the mold of many books. You see the marks of fires which have swept along these mountain sides; here and there the trunk of a redwood has been streaked by a tongue of flame. But the tree wears its crown of eternal green. It is only the dry sticks and rubbish which are burned up to make more room for the giants; while many noxious reptiles have been driven back to their holes. Possibly, the wood-ticks number some millions less. But very little that is worth saving is consumed.

We shall need a regenerating fire some day, to do for books what is done for the forests. May it be a hot one when it comes. Let no dry sticks nor vermin escape. Ninety in every hundred books which have got into our libraries within the last half century, will fail to enlighten the world until there is one good, honest conflagration. Something might be gained from the ashes of these barren books; therefore, pile on the rubbish, and use the poker freely. Let not the fire go out until some cords of pious doggerel, concocted in the name of poetry, have been added thereto. The giants will survive the flames; but punk-wood, moths, and wood-ticks will all be gone.

By a noteworthy coincidence, when the smell of autumn fruits comes up from the valley, and the grapes hang in clusters on the hillsides, and wine-presses over-flow, the last sign of dearth is obliterated by the swelling of all hidden fountains. The earth is not jubilant without water. The springs which had been lost, gurgle in the crevices of the rocks, and streaks of dampness are seen along the trails, where, in the early morning, little rivulets ran and interlaced and retired before the sun. There will be no rain for weeks. There has been none for months. The trees by the wayside faint and droop under the burden of heat and dust. But they know this signal of the coming rain. The fountains below seem to know, also, at what time the fountains above are to be unsealed; and these pulsing streams are the answer-ing signal. Shorter days and diminished solar evaporation will answer as a partial clearing up of the mystery. But if the profoundest truth has not yet been touched, suppose, oh philosopher of many books and many doubts, that you let your grap-nel into the depths for it? Only be sure that your line is long enough, and that you bring no more rubbish to the surface. There is more truth above ground than most of us will master. And we stumble over it in field and forest, like luckless treasure-hunters; when a ringing blow upon the dull rock would reveal filaments of gold, or the glancing light of crystals. There are some truths, also, whose insuf-ferable light we cannot bear. They must be shaded off, like half tints at set of sun. And if any prophet coming out of the wilderness shall dare to tell more, let him eat his locusts and wild honey first, for he cannot tell whether he will be crowned or stoned.

A WEEK IN MENDOCINO.

IF one is in robust health and a vigorous trencher-man, who is there on the earth, in these degenerate times, to congratulate him on such good fortune? But no sooner is there a gastric revolt at the diabolical inventions of some high-priestess of the kitchen, with a growing cadaverousness, than every friend is ready with an ominous warning. When we publish a list of the patent medicines recommended, the world will know how many disinterested friends we have. Just now, the earth cure is all-potent. Try it in any shape you like—as a mud bath, a powder, a poultice, or an honest bed at mid-day—and this chemistry of earth and sun will work wonders. Are we not getting back to first principles? You talk of the shaking up which religious dogmas have suffered within the last half century: what is there of all the medical theories of the last fifteen hundred years which now goes unchallenged?

Yosemite has been a little overdone of late. The seashore and the springs are dreadfully haunted by the young lady in rustic hat, garnished with pea-green ribbon, and who either writes poetry, or reads the latest love story. There is comfort in the fact that the territory of this State is not more than half explored, and is not likely to be for some time to come. There are reaches equal to a degree of latitude untrodden, as yet, by the foot of the tourist, and where the clanking of the surveyor's chain and rods has never been heard; and some of these you may find within two hundred miles of San Francisco. Going still farther, there are vales where a white man was, till recently, something of a curiosity. It is interesting to find a country where morganatic marriages are in high repute. The red-headed lumberman's cross-cut saw would not, by this arrangement, descend to his children; nor would an old hunter's powder-horn and ancient rifle, by the same prudential forethought, be handed down to some little vagabond half-breeds.

In twenty-four hours one may be set down in the wildest part of Mendocino County. We selected Anderson Valley, on the headwaters of the Novarro River, not so much for its wildness as because it was the most accessible spot unfrequented by the tourist. It will be hard to miss the Russian River Valley in getting there, and harder still not to linger for a day or two to look at such pictures as no artist has quite succeeded in putting on to his canvas.

There was the mid-day repose of St. Helena, taking on a royal purple as the day advanced; the droning sound of the reapers in the valley, as the rippling wheat bowed to a sort of rural song of Old Hundred! and the very cattle, which, for aught I know, have figured in a dozen pictures, standing under the trees, with their identical tails over their backs. Even the great fields of corn, which rustled and snapped under a midsummer sun, were toned a little by the long column of mellow dust which spun from the stage-wheels and trailed for a mile in the rear. The artists caution against too much green in a picture, and so this brown pigment was needed to give the best effect; and there was no lack of material to "lay it on" liberally, anywhere in that region. With the dropping down of the sun behind the low hills on the west, the shadows fell aslant the valley, and light and shade melted together into the soft twilight. It might have been a favorable time for sentiment. But just then the stage-coach rounded a low hillock, and a farm-house was brought suddenly into the foreground. A cosset, a flock of geese, a windmill moving its fans indolently to the breath of the west wind, a dozen ruminating cows—what more of pastoral simplicity would you have for the fringe of such a landscape? But you see it was slightly overdone. The stout young woman milking the roan cow rather heightened the effect, to be sure; she really ought to have been there. But did any feminine mortal ever administer such a kick to the broad sides of a cow before? There was a dull thud, a quadrupedal humping, an undulation along the spine of that cow—and the stage-coach was out of sight. O, for the brawn and muscle to administer such a kick! It was more gymnastic than esthetic, more realistic than poetical. You will never find Arcadia where such a powerful feminine battery is set in motion on so slight a provocation. A cow might survive; but you need not describe the fate of any man on whom such a force were expended. And seeing that so large a part of this world needs a healthy kicking, more is the pity that there should have been such a needless expenditure of force. By what mental law are grand and ridiculous scenes associated together? I cannot summon the towering majesty of St. Helena, the golden ripple of the harvest fields, the receding valley, softened by the twilight, but ever in the foreground is this kicking milkmaid and that unfortunate cow. If a house-painter had dabbed his brush of green paint on your Van Dyke, you might be stunned by this very audacity, and turn your pet picture to the wall. But the house-painter and Van Dyke would from that time forth be associated together. So I turn this picture to the wall, only wishing that the kicking milkmaid and St. Helena had been a thousand miles apart.

The Russian River Valley "pinches out" at Cloverdale, a pretty little town, set down in a bowl with a very large rim—so large, that unless new life should be infused into the town, it will not be likely to slop over. Thence, you reach the head of Anderson Valley, by a jaunt of thirty-two miles, in a northwesterly direction, over a series of low mountain ridges, and through canyons, sometimes widening out into "potreros" large enough for a cattle ranch, and handsome enough for a gentlemen's country-seat. Here the affluents of the Novarro River are drawn together like threads of lace; and the first trout stream leaps and eddies in the deep defiles on its way to the ocean. There is no use of fumbling in an outside pocket for fish-hooks. The stream has a fishy look; but that band of rancheria Indians, who have gone into summer camp on a sand-bar, will settle the trout question for the next ten miles. They pop their heads out of a round hole in one of the wigwams like prairie dogs, and seem to stand on their hind legs, with the others pendent, as if just going to bark. These are the aboriginal Gypsies, fortunate rascals, who pay no house-rent, who want nothing but what they can steal, or what can be got from the brawling stream, or the wooded slopes of the adjacent hills.

These funnel-shaped willow baskets, lodged here and there along the banks, are the salmon traps of the Indians, which have done duty until the spring run was over. When the salmon has once set his head up stream, he never turns it down again until he has reached the extreme limits of his journey and accomplished his destiny. The Indians understand this; and these long willow funnels, with a bell-shaped mouth, are laid down in the spring—a clumsy contrivance to be sure; but the salmon enters and pushes his way on, while this willow cylinder contracts until it closes to a small nozzle. There is daylight ahead; the stubborn fish will not back down, and he cannot "move on." When an Indian gets hungry, he pulls up this willow trap, runs a spit through his fish, holds him over the fire a little while, and his dinner is ready.

There is no fish story which one may not believe when in a gentle mood. And thus, when farther down the stream, a settler showed us a wooden fork such as is used to load gavels of grain, with which, in less than an hour, he pitched out of this same stream a wagon-load of salmon—why should we doubt his veracity? No lover of the gentle art is ever skeptical about the truth of a fish story. Faith and good luck go together. How was our faith rewarded soon afterward, when, taking a "cut-off," at the first cast under a shelving rock, a half-pound trout was landed! It was a grasshopper bait, and another grasshopper had to be run down before another cast. It is wonderful what jumps this insect will make when he is wanted for bait, and the run is up the hill. Another trout snapped illusively, and we had him—larger by a quarter of a pound than the first. It was getting interesting! No doubt the settler pitched out a load of salmon with a wooden fork. A kingdom for a grasshopper! There they go in all directions—and the rascals have wings! The clumsy stage-wagon is creeping far up the hill. A beetle is tried; it won't do—no decent trout ever swallowed a beetle. A dozen splendid game fish were left in that swirl under the rock. Was there too much faith in that wooden fork story, or not enough? There was a hitch somewhere. But it was all right when the passengers dined that day on fried bacon, and we on mountain trout. If the grasshoppers had not been too lively, there would have been trout for all.

Anderson Valley is about eighteen miles long, and half to three-fourths of a mile wide. The hills on the left are belted with a heavy growth of redwood, in fine contrast with the treeless hills on the right, covered with a heavy crop of wild oats, all golden-hued in the August sun. The farms extend across the valley, taking a portion of the hills on either side. There has not been a Government survey made in the valley, but every man was in possession of his own, and did not covet his neighbor's. Land-stealing requires a degree of energetic rascality and enterprise wholly wanting here. So near, and yet so remote! It is as if one had gone a two-days' journey, and had somehow managed to get three thousand miles away. I heard of a man in the valley who took a newspaper, and was disposed to sympathize with him in his misfortune. Why should the spray of one of the dirty surges of the outside world break over into Arcadia? Everybody had enough, and nobody had anything in particular to do. The dwellings had mud-and-stick chimneys on the outside, and an occasional bake-oven garnished the back yard. At the little tavern, such vegetables as strangers "hankered for" were procured at the coast—a distance of twenty-six miles. An old man—he might have been seventy, with a margin of twenty years—had heard of the rebellion, and lamented the abolition of slavery—a mischief which he attributed to a few fanatics. The world would never get on smoothly until the institution of the patriarchs had been restored.

Oh, venerable friend, dwelling in Arcadia! there is much broken pottery in this world which is past all mending; and more which is awaiting its turn to go into the rubbish heap. All that was discovered in the interior of a Western mound was a few fragments of earthenware; for the rest, Time had beaten it all back to the dust. The images, whether of brass, wood, or stone, could not be put together by any of the cohesive arts of our time. It is appointed for some men to go through the world, club in hand, and to break much of the world's crockery as they go. We may not altogether like them. But observe that the men who are stoned by one generation are canonized by the next. There was the great ebony image set up and so long worshipped by the people of this country. How many sleek, fat doctors climbed into their pulpits of a Sunday, to expatiate on the scriptural beauties of this image, and the duty of reverencing it as something set up and continued by Divine authority! It took some whacking blows to bring that ebony idol down; but what a world of hypocrisy, cruelty and lies went into the dust with it! Was there ever a reformer—a genuine image-breaker—who did not, at one time or another, make the world howl with rage and pain? Now, truth is on eternal foundations, and does not suffer, in the long run, by the world's questionings or buffetings. But a consecrated falsehood—whether sacerdotal, political, or social—is some day smitten, as the giant of old, in the forehead, and falls headlong. After all, it is by revolution, that the world makes most of its progress. It is a violent and often disorderly going out of an old and dead condition by the regenerating power, not of a new truth, but of an old one dug out of the rubbish, and freshly applied to the conscience of the world. How many truths to-day lie buried, which, if dug up, would set the world in an uproar! The image-breaker often heralds a revolution. He overturns the idol, of whatever sort it is, letting the light into some consecrated falsehood—not gently, but very rudely, and with a shocking disregard of good manners, as many affirm. This rough-shod evangel, with the rasping voice, and angular features, and pungent words—we neither like him nor his new gospel at first. But he improves on acquaintance, and some day we begin to doubt whether he really does deserve eternal burning.

The world is full of cant; it infects our common speech. The odor of sanctity and the form of sound words are no nearer the living spirit than are those petrifactions which present an outline of men, but never again pulsate with life. Once in every half a century it is needful that the image-breaker should come along and knock on the head the brainless images of cant. The sturdy man of truthful and resolute speech! How irreverent and impious he is! He makes the timid hold their breath, lest he should break something that he ought not to touch. What has he done, after all, but to teach men and women to be more truthful, more courageous, and less in love with shams.

At the close of a little "exhortation," something like this, the old man said—rather dogmatically, I thought—"Stranger, them sentiments of yourn won't do for this settlement." No doubt he was right. They won't do for any settlement where they build mud-and-stick chimneys on the outside of houses, and fry meat within.

It is good to get into a forest where there is not a mark of the woodman's axe. The redwood is, after all, one of the handsomest coniferous trees in the world. It grows only in a good soil and a moist climate. There may be larger trees of the *sequoia* family in the Calaveras group, but that presumption will bear questioning. A guide offered to take us to a group of trees, distant about a day's ride, the largest of which he affirmed was seventy-five feet in circumference, and not less than two hundred and sixty feet high. Larger trees than this are reported in the Coast Range; but we have never yet *seen* a redwood which measured over fifty feet in circumference, nor can any considerable tree of this species be found beyond the region of sandstone and the belt of coast fogs.

It is curious to note tree and tribal limitations. The oak and the redwood do not associate together, but the madrono is the friend of both. The line of redwood limits the habitation of the ground squirrel, and within that line his half-brother, the wood squirrel, arches his tail in the overhanging boughs, and barks just when the charge is out of your gun, with surprising impudence. There is the dominion of trees and animals older and better defined than any law of boundaries which has yet got into our statute-books. Who knows but races of men have overleaped boundaries of Divine ordination, and so must struggle with adverse fate towards nothing more hopeful than extinction. The black man of the tropics, planted near the North Pole, has all the grin taken out of him, and there is nothing but a frigid chatter left. There is the Indian of the great central plains. Have we got into his country, or has he got into ours? There is some confusion of boundaries; and the locomotive, that demon of modern civilization, is tracing new boundaries with a trail of fire. It is possible to put one's finger upon the weak link in the logic that what is bad for the Indian is good for the white man.

That gopher snake just passed on the trail, with a young rabbit half swallowed, illustrates near enough how one-half of the world is trying to swallow the other. Observe, too, that provision of nature, by which game is swallowed larger than the throat. It is the smallest half of the world, it seems, that is trying to swallow the largest half, with good prospect of success. Half a dozen men have located all the redwood timber upon the accessible streams of this county. Looking coastward along the Novarro, there is a chain of townships spanning this stream for fifteen miles in length, owned by two men. You may write down the names of twenty men who are at this moment planning to swallow all the leading business interests of this State. They will elect Governors and Legislators. It don't matter that the game is larger than the throat. In fact, deglutition is already pretty well advanced—as far, at least, as with the rabbit; but with this difference, that our victims will be made to grease themselves.

If the day is preceded by three or four hours of moonlight, you will not often find a deer browsing after the sun is up. His work is done, and he has lain down in a thicket for a morning nap. It was kind of the log-driver to take us to the hills at the faintest streak of dawn. But once there, he slipped away by himself, and in hardly more than half an hour there were three cracks of a rifle. He came round with no game. We had seen none. It was not so very interesting to stand as a sentinel on the hill-tops in the chill of a gray morning, yearning for one's breakfast, and wishing all the deer were locked up in some canyon with a bottomless abyss. A new stand was taken, when presently our friend pointed out the line of a deer's back, standing half hidden by a clump of rocks of nearly the same color. We must both fire together, and make a sure thing of the game. There was a sharp report, and the deer jumped clear of the rocks and disappeared. He fell in his tracks. There was a single bullet-mark. But our friend insisted that both shots had taken effect in the same spot. It was a fawn, not more than two-thirds grown, and the glaze was just coming over its mild, beseeching eyes. We were sorry for a moment that both rifles had not missed. The log-driver shouldered the game, but disclaimed all ownership. A little farther on a dead buck was skewered over a limb, and still farther a buck and a doe were suspended in the same way. It was a good morning's work. Every shot of the log-driver had told. A slight pang of remorse was succeeded by a little glow of exultation. Venison is good, and a hungry man is carnivorous. It is a clear case that the taking of this one deer is right. The log-driver must satisfy his conscience for taking three, as best he can. His left eye had a merry twinkle, however, when, on handing over our gun, he observed that the cap only had exploded, and that the load placed there on setting out was still in the rifle chamber. Well, we got the venison, and the log-driver told his sly story with a keen relish, and some addenda.

This Arcadia is a wondrously human place, after all. Borrowing a pony to ride up the valley three or four miles, night and the hospitality of a neighbor overtook us. A mist settled down over the valley, and under the great overhanging trees not a trace of the road could be seen. "Only give him the rein," said the settler, "and the horse will go straight home." We gave him the rein. An hour, by guess, had gone by, and still that pony was ambling along, snorting occasionally as the dry sticks broke suspiciously in the edge of the woods. If a grizzly was there, his company was not wanted. Another hour had gone by. Pray, how long does it take a pony to amble over three miles in a pitch-dark night? Half an hour later, he turned off to the left, crossed the valley, and brought up at a fence. "Give him the rein," was the injunction. He had that, and a vigorous dig besides. In half an hour more he was on the other side of the valley, drawn up at another fence. It was too dark to discover any house. The true destination was a small white tavern by the roadside, and the light of the wood fire in the great fire-place would certainly shine through the window. The vagabond pony took the spur viciously, and went off under the trees. We were lost; that was certain. It was getting toward midnight. It was clear that this equine rascal was not going home. He had traveled at least four hours, and was now, probably, several miles outside the settlement, unless he had been going around in a circle. A night in a wilderness, enveloped in a chilling fog, the moisture of which was now dripping from the trees, with the darkness too great to discover when the horse laid his ears back as a sign of danger, was the best thing in prospect. Some time afterward he had evidently turned into a field, and a few minutes later was in front of a settler's house. A ferocious dog made it useless to dismount; the bars were jumped—the diminutive cob coming down on his knees, and a moment afterward bringing up under the window of a small house. The window went up slowly, in answer to a strong midnight salutation; and to this day it is not quite clear whether a rifle barrel, a pitchfork, or a hoe-handle was protruded from that window, or whether all this was an illusion born of the darkness of the night.

"Well, stranger, how did you get in here, and what do you want?" asked the keeper of this rural castle.

"I am lost; you must either let me in, or come out and show me the way."

"Likely story you're lost! Reckon that don't go down in this settlement. You ain't lost if you're here, are you?"

"Look here! I borrowed Jimson's pony to go up to Dolman's, and started back after nightfall. Dolman said, 'Give him the reign, and he would go straight back to the tavern.' I gave him the rein, and he has been going for the last four or five hours, except when he stopped two or three times at fences, until he brought up here."

I think the hoe-handle, or whatever it might have been, was slowly drawn in. A match was touched off on the casement, making about as much light as a fire-fly. The settler, shading his eyes, threw a glimmer of light on to the neck of the iron-gray pony.

"Yes; that's Jimson's pony—that are a fact."

A moment after, a tall figure glided out, as from a hole in the wall, and stood by the horse.

"Now, tell me, my good friend, where I am, what is the hour, and how to get back to the tavern."

"Well, it mought be nigh onto twelve o'clock, and you're not more'n two miles from Jimson's."

"I left at seven o'clock to go down to Jimson's, about three miles. Where have I been all this time? If I have been nearly five hours going half of three miles, how shall I ever get back to the tavern?"

"Stranger, you don't understand all the ways of this settlement. You see that's the pony that the Jimson boys take when they go 'round courting the gals in this valley. He thought you wanted to go 'round kind o' on a lark; and that pony, for mere devilment, had just as lief go-a-courting as not. Stopped out yonder at a fence, did he, and then went across the valley, and then over to the foot-hills? Well, he went up to Tanwood's first, and being as that didn't suit, expect he went across to Weatherman's—he's got a fine gal—then he came on down to Jennings'—mighty fine gal there. He's been there with the boys lots o' times."

"Well, why did the pony come over here?"

"You see, stranger, I've got a darter, too."

"How far has that wandering rascal carried me since seven o'clock?"

"Nigh upon fifteen miles, maybe twenty; and he'd a gone all night, if you'd let him. He ain't half done the settlement yet."

"Then I, a middle-aged man of family, have been carried 'round this settlement in this fog, which goes to the marrow-bones, and under trees, to get a broken head, and on blind cross-trails, for twenty miles or so, and have got just half-way back; and all because this pony is used by the boys for larking?"

"I reckon you've struck it, stranger. Mustn't blame that hoss too much. He thought you was on it. Now, it's a straight road down to Jimson's; but don't let him turn to the left below. Runnel lives down there, and he's got a darter, too. She's a smart 'un."

A few minutes later, as if the evil one was in that iron-gray, he took the left-hand road. But he sprang to the right, when the rowel went into his flank, carrying with it the assurance that the game was up.

It was past midnight when that larking pony came steaming up to the little white tavern. The smoldering wood fire threw a flickering light into the porch, enough to see that the ears of the gamy little horse were set forward in a frolicking way, saying clearly enough: "If you had only given me the rein, as advised, we would have made a night of it."

This new Arcadia is not so dull, when once the ways are learned. The Jimson boys affirmed that the pony was just mean enough to play such a trick on a stranger. But the old tavern loft rang with merriment until the small hours of the night. It was moderated by a motherly voice which came from the foot of the stairs: "You had better hush up. The stranger knows all the places where you've been gallivanting 'round this settlement."

When the sun had just touched the hills with a morning glory, we were well on the way out of the valley. Coveys of quails with half-grown chicks were coming out from cover. The grouse were already at work in the wild berry patches on the side of the mountain; one or two larks went before with an opening benediction, while the glistening madrono shed its shower of crystals. Looking back, there was a thin, blue vapor curling up from the cabins. We were reconciled to the mud-and-stick chimneys on the outside, with a reservation about the fried meat within. Peace be with the old man who said our speech would not do for that settlement. And long life to the pony that mistook our sober mission for one of wooing and frolic on a dark and foggy night.

UNDER A MADROÑO.

JEEHEEBOY, the Parsee, says that the highest conception of heaven is a place where there is nothing to do. We had found that place under an oak, yesterday, and had conquered a great peace. All the world was going right, for once, no matter which way it went. But opening one eye, the filagree of sunlight, sifting through the leaves, disclosed hundreds of worms letting themselves down by gossamer cables toward the earth. Now and then a swallow darted under the tree, and left a cable fluttering without ballast in the breeze. If a worm is ambitious to plumb some part of the universe, there is no philosophy in this world which will insure perfect composure, when it is clear that one's nose or mouth is to be made the "objective point." The madrono harbors no vagabonds—not a leaf is punctured, and no larva is deposited under its bark, probably for the reason that the outer rind is thrown off every year. It is not kingly, but it is the one undefiled tree of the forest. When its red berries are ripe, the robins have a thanksgiving-day; and the shy wild pigeons dart among its branches, unconsciously making themselves savory for the spit.

Little creepers of *yerba buena*—the sweetest and most consoling of all herbs—interlace underneath the tree; and within sight the dandelion blooms, and perfects its juices for some torpid liver; while under the fence the wild sage puts forth its gray leaves, gathering subtile influences from earth and air to give increase of wisdom and longevity. If the motherly old prophetess of other days—she who had such faith in God and simples—would come this way, she might gather herbs enough to cure no small part of this disordered world.

Take it all in all, one might go a long way and not find another more perfect landscape. The dim, encircling mountains—one with the ragged edges of an extinct volcano still visible; the warm hill-sides, where vine, and fig, and olive blend; the natural park in the foreground, begirt with clear waters which break through a canyon above—the home of trout, grown too cunning for the hook, except on cloudy days; the line of perpetual green which the rivulet carries a mile farther down, and loses it at the fretting shore line; the village, with its smart obtrusiveness toned by distance; and the infinite reach of the ocean beyond—these all enter into the composition. Well, if one has a "stake in the soil" just here, what is the harm in coming to drive it a little once a year, and to enjoy the luxury of wiping out such scores as are run up on the debit side of the account? Farming for dividends is a prosy business; but farming with a discount may have a world of sentiment in it.

Have you quite answered the question yet, whether the instinct of certain animals is not reason? Here are a dozen quadrupedal friends that can demonstrate the fact that they have something more than instinct. There is that honest old roan horse coming from the side-hill for his lump of sugar. He knows well enough that he is not entitled to it now. He is only coming to try his chances. But give him an hour under the saddle, then turn him out and see if he will not get it. Forgetting once to give him his parting lump, he came back again at midnight from the field, and, thrusting his head into an open window, whinnied such a blast that every inmate of the farm-house bolted from bed. He got his sugar, but with a look of injured innocence; and ever since has been dealt with in good faith. Charley is something of a sportsman, in his way. In the autumn you have only to get on his back with a gun, and he trudges off to places where the quails come out from covert by hundreds into the little openings in the chaparral. The horse will edge up very near to them; when he drops his head, that is his signal to fire. If lithe enough, you will pick them up without leaving the saddle. If you get down to gather up the game he will wait. He will go on in his own way, and discover the birds long before you can, dropping his head as a signal at just the right moment. You may call this horse sense, but it is horse reason—so near akin to human reason that there might be some trouble in tracing the dividing line. So much for this old cob, who smuggles his honest head under your coat for sugar, knowing well enough that he has not earned it.

Another horse, now dead and happy, I hope, in the other world, stopped one dark night, when half-way down a steep and dangerous hill. There was a neighbor, with wife and babies, in the carriage. The horse would not budge an inch (not under the whip), but turned his head around, declaring, as plainly as a horse could, that there was danger. The hold-back straps had broken, and the pressure of the carriage against his haunches, which sustained the entire load from the top of the hill, had started the blood cruelly; yet there he stood, resolutely holding back wife and babies from destruction, choosing even to suffer the indignities of the lash, rather than that injury should come to one of his precious charge. Did that horse have reason? I rather think so; and that he only needed articulation to have made a remonstrance quite as much to the point as that memorable one made by Balaam's ass.

There is that great mastiff, yawning so lazily, with power to hold an ox at his will, or to throttle a man. But no man could abuse him as that little child does every day. He understands well enough that that lump of animated dough has not arrived at years of discretion, and so he submits to all manner of cruelties with perfect patience. How, with mere instinct, does he find out that this child is not yet a "moral agent," and that all these pinchings, and pluckings, and brandings with a hot poker are the irresponsible freaks of the young rascal, who can get off harmless by pleading the Baby Act? This honest dog would die for that little child who abuses him every day. But let a "Greaser" come to take so much as one Brahma pullet from the roost, and he has him by the throat. Does instinct account for this clear perception of right and wrong?

Some clever ways he has, also, of winning favor. He has got it into his head that a certain black cat, that sleeps in any little patch of sunlight on the kitchen floor, is a nuisance, and he has taken a contract to abate it. But, at the same time, he is on such friendly terms with pussy that he would not hurt her for the world.

Now a cat knows, by instinct, how to carry her kittens and not hurt them. But how did this dog find out that a cat can be carried safely and comfortably by the nape of her neck? Very gently he takes up pussy thus by her neck, carries her off a quarter of a mile or so from the farm-house, sets her down, and then comes back and balances the account with a crust of bread, or any odd fragment of meat, by way of lunch. On one occasion puss got back to the house before him. It bothered him that the case amounted so nearly to a "breach of contract." Taking puss once more by the neck, he carried her across a creek, and, setting her down on the other side, returned with an air of profound satisfaction. He got an extra lunch that day. But how did the dog know that a cat has a mortal aversion to crossing a stream of water? If that dog had no more than mere instinct, pray, what is reason?

His "predecessor" was a foolish dog, not more than "half-witted." But even his canine idiocy gave way to gleams of reason. He became an expert at driving cattle which trespassed on the farm. If the herd scattered, he singled out the leader, laid hold of his tail, and steered him as well as a yachtman could steer his craft through an intricate channel. After two or three steers had been piloted in this way, the rest would follow the leaders. The dog had hit upon the most economical plan with respect to time and the distance to be traversed. But, one day, in managing a vicious mustang-ox, his patience was sorely tried. Jerking him suddenly into the right path, his tail parted! The whole bovine steering-apparatus had given way, as completely as a ship's rudder in a storm. The dog never could quite comprehend the case. He took himself to his kennel, and would never drive cattle afterward. In fact, he was never the same dog after that catastrophe. Only instinct, you say? But then, if there had been an asylum for canine idiots, that dog would have been entitled to a ticket of admission. His exceptional foolishness confirms our theory.

Years ago, a seven-year-old brought home an insignificant little mongrel—a mere puppy—and pleaded so earnestly for its toleration that the maternal judgment was quite overcome. "Chip" was always a nuisance, but understood more of human speech than any dog "on record." If the plans of the day were discussed in his hearing, he comprehended the principal movements to be made. If the plan excluded his company he knew it, and stole away a half-hour in advance, always selecting the right road, and putting in his mute plea for forbearance in just the nick of time to make it available. Half a dozen times was that dog given away. Yet he always knew the day on which the transfer was to be made, and on that particular day he could never be found. Now, does a dog that understands the significance of human speech, without a motion or gesture—not only interpreting but connecting a series of ideas, so as to comprehend, in advance, plans and movements—find out all these things by mere instinct? You may limit and qualify the term, but it is reason, after all.

Train a fox ever so much, and you cannot develop anything in him but the meanest instincts. He will never be grateful, and never honest, nor can any terms of friendship be established with him. His traditional cunning is a hateful dishonesty. After nearly a year of tuition on a young gray fox, he was never advanced to any respectable degree of intelligence. He would lie at the mouth of his kennel for hours to confiscate any old hen who happened to pass with a brood of chickens, disdaining, the while, to seize any plump young rooster that passed within reach, because his diabolical instinct was to work the greatest possible amount of mischief. After making a hundred young chickens orphans, he broke his chain one night and left for the forest. The thief came back a few nights afterward to make more orphans. That gray pelt tacked up on the rear of the barn is his obituary.

A series of brilliant experiments that were to have been made on a young rattlesnake turned out not a whit more satisfactory. The reptile was not "raised" just here, but was presented by a friend. His teeth were to have been drawn, after which various observations were to have been made concerning his tastes and habits, and particularly his disposition when not provoked. There was a prospect of making an honest reptile of him. He was put in an empty barrel for the night; but next morning two half-breed Shanghaes had him, one by the tail and the other by the head. He parted about midway, each miserable rooster swallowing his half, and that without even the excuse of a morbid appetite. Since that time I have never been able to hate a young rattlesnake half as much as that detestable breed of Shanghaes.

If one is not sick unto death, what more effectual medication can be found than the sun, and the south wind, and the all-embracing earth? The children of the poor are healthy, because they sprout out of the very dirt. The sun dispels humors, enriches the blood; and the winds execute a sanitary commission for these neglected ones. They live because they are of the earth—earthy. The experiment of training a race of attenuated cherubs in the shade, and making them martyrs to clean aprons and clean dickeys, is a failure. There is a vast amount of *post mortem* doggerel that never would have been written if the cherubs had only made dirt-pies, and had eaten freely of them. Observe the strong tendency in men, even of culture, to court the wildness and rude energy of savage life. Let one sleep on the ground, in a mild climate, for three months, and even the man who reads Homer is content, often, to sleep there the rest of his lifetime. It is better to tame the savage rather cautiously, and with some reserve, for if he be eliminated wholly, the best relations with Nature are broken off. Evermore we are seeking for something among books and pictures, and in the babblings of polite society, that we do not find. When the blood is thin, and the body has become spiritualized, then it is easy to ascend to the clouds, as balloons go up, and hold high discourse; while the world, under our feet, teeming with its myriad lives, pulsating even to the smallest dust, and all glorified, if we will behold it, is not taken into fellowship, its speech interpreted nor its remedial forces marshaled as friends, to back our halting and troubled humanity. It has taken almost six thousand years to find out that a handful of dry earth will heal the most cruel wound. In the day of our mortal hurt we do but go back to the earth, believing that in the ages to come we shall go forth again, eternally renewed.

There are islands in the Pacific where birds and beasts, and every living thing, are free from fear of, or even a suspicion of wrong, from man. But where civilization is introduced, there is a bridgeless gulf between us and all orders of existence beneath. There is a half-articulate protest coming up, that this thing called modern civilization is treacherous, cruel, and dishonest. For a century its evangels have proclaimed its mission of love. But humanity has wrestled with its own kind more fiercely than ever before. It is decent enough to kill each other, if done according to some conventional code. But it is vulgar to eat our enemies; and so the custom, in polite society, has fallen into disuse.

Is it a wonder that all animate nature is accusatory and suspicious? Little by little we win it back to our confidence. The birds that were silent and moody, because of our intrusion, give, after a while, little fragments of song, and hop down on the lower branches, holding inquisitory councils. A lizard runs along upon a fallen tree, each time getting a little nearer; he has the handsomest of eyes, but not a good facial expression; yet so lithe and nimble, and improves so on acquaintance that we shall soon be friends. Darting his tongue through an insect, he comes a little nearer, as though he would ask, "Do you take your prey in that way?" Two orioles have swung up their hammock to the swaying branch of a chestnut oak. They do not swing from the madrono, because its branches are too stiff and un-yielding. They have been in trouble for half an hour. The robins were in trouble earlier in the day; a dozen of them went after a butcher-bird, and whipped him honestly and handsomely. There is a little brown owl, sitting on a dry limb, not a hundred yards off. He came into the world with a sort of antediluvian gravity that never bodes any good. If the solemn bird could only sing, he would allay suspicion at once. Never has a song-bird a bloody beak. Your solemn-visaged men of frigid propriety, out of whose joyless natures a song or a laugh never breaks, can thrust their talons into human prey, if but occasion only serve, as this owl will into some poor bird just at the going down of the sun.

The bees come and go sluggishly, either because there is an opiate in the sweets of the wild poppy, which flames on the hill-side, or because there is no winter season here demanding great reserves of honey. Nearly all of them turn vagabonds and robbers in this country. The line of departure is toward a redwood, which is dry at the top, a knot-hole evidently serving for ingress and egress. If their own stores fail, they will go to some tame hive and fight their more honest neighbors and plunder all their reserves. Even a bee-hive is no longer a symbol of lawful industry, since the bees have become knaves, and do not even rob in a chivalrous way. But they, in turn, will be despoiled by some vagabond who has carved his initials on every "suspected" tree hereabout. It is a world of reprisals after all. The strong prey upon the weak; and they, in turn, after passing virtuous resolutions of indignant dissent, spoil those who are weaker still. It is a hard necessity. But how can the fox do without the hare, the hawk without a thrush, or he without a beetle, or the beetle without his fly? Strong nations capture the weak; and there are weak and pitiful races of men, with no force or vitality to found nations and dynasties. These only wait to be plucked up by the stronger, as so much human rubbish waiting for flood and flame. High-breeding may degenerate races. Your thoroughbred cattle, however, take the premiums at the great fairs of the world. It is not necessary that the ancestral pedigree should be a long one. But so far as men and women are thoroughbred with respect to muscle and brain, will they, consciously or otherwise, carry with them the sceptre of dominion and conquest. They will crowd out inferior races, either by sheer force or by some trick of diplomacy. An Indian exchanging territory for blankets, or sending his arrow against an iron-clad, finds it a losing business always. We write him up handsomely in romances, but extinguish him cruelly with rifle and sabre.

There was a halo lingering about the dome of the old Mission Church, in the distance; its cross was glorified just before the sun rested its disk upon the ocean. The hard outlines of the mountains softened, and took on a purple hue; the white doves came down out of the clouds, and clustered about the gables; a light flickered like a fire-fly in the light-house half a league beyond the church, and another from a window of the farm-house near by. That skipper, wide off, may take his bearings from the light on the shore. But at night-fall, the wide-spreading roof is more hospitable that even this branching madrono. And there is no philosophy that could not be improved by June butter, redolent of white clover, with a supplement of cream half an inch thick.

A DAY ON THE LOS GATOS.

THE brightest stream which bubbles out of the mountains in the Coast Range, and loses itself on the plains of Santa Clara, ought to have had a more poetical name. Its feline etymology is probably owing to the fact that as many wild cats rendezvous about its headwaters as are congregated within the same limits in any place on these mountain-slopes. This superabundance of savage life, which so incontinently runs to white teeth and claws, is an indication that there is much game in this region. Pussy likes a good bill of fare, and makes it up of hares, cotton-tail rabbits, ground-squirrels, quails, doves, and a great number of singing birds, not omitting an occasional rattlesnake, which is killed so deftly that there is no chance for a venomous bite. If the unlovely creatures had been more industrious in this line, the thrushes would have had a better chance, and that dry, reedy sound in the brush—the one drawback to the pleasure of crawling on all-fours through the chaparral—would not have started a cold chill along the spine quite so often.

That little square-looking dog, loaned by a settler at the foot of the mountain, with his ears split in a dozen places in his encounters with these animals, goes along for the fun and excitement of another clinch with his old enemy. The warfare is, after all, conducted on scientific principles. The wild cat is as strong as a young tiger, and you see by the depth of the shoulders and the size of the head, that he will fight terribly. He does not run well, and cannot catch a hare in any other way than by stealth. The dog runs him to a tree; the cat ascends to the highest strong limb, goes out on that, and gets an adjustment by which the smallest possible mark will be presented for a rifle or pistol-shot. If you want to do the handsome thing, let the head alone; for that is well defended by the limb on which it is resting. The wind blowing strong at an oblique angle to your line, will make a difference of at least an inch in sending that light ball 180 feet; it will also drop from a right ascending line nearly two inches. Remember, a shrewd woodsman never forgets these things. Getting your margin adjusted, plant the ball into the shoulder, just under the spine. He will drop from the tree with only one foreleg in fighting condition. The dog is on his back in a second, and there will be the liveliest rough-and-tumble fight you have seen in many a day. Never mind the wild screams that echo from the canyon. That fellow's time has come. He will not steal your best game-chicken out of the top of the tree again.

The dog has won the battle; but he has got some ugly scars along his sides and flank. Observe that, overheated as he is, he does not rush into that clear stream. He takes his bath in that shallow spring with a soft mud bottom. Note how he plasters himself, laying the wounded side underneath, and then, setting down on his haunches, buries all the wounded parts in the ooze. The mud has medicinal properties. The dog knows it. No physician could make so good a poultice for the wounds of a cat's claws as this dog has made for himself. Pray, if you had been clawed in that way by either feline or feminine, would you have found anything at the bottom of your book philosophy so remedial as this dog has found.

Now that this striped rascal has had his light put out, it is hard to justify the act after all. He was a thief, stealthy, cowardly, blood-loving, and cruel. But then his education had been neglected. And while his moral sentiments had been lapsing for generations, note what a gain there has been in his animal development; for he is next of kin to the common house-cat. You cannot upset this theory by pointing to his abbreviated tail. How long do you suppose it is since every one of your hair-splitting casuists had a tail more than twice as long as this fellow, whose descendants, in two generations more, may have none at all? Taking him up by his enormous jowls, rounding off a head suggesting diabolical acquisitiveness, it is only necessary to carry a Darwinian rush-light in the other hand to go straight to the right man and say: Here is a link in your chain of development, only three removes from the point you have reached. What a pity that this diminution of tail and claws does not signify a corresponding decrease of cruel and stealthy circumvention! You wag your tail approvingly to this proposition, Samson. But this business of exterminating pests had better cease. Because, if carried out honestly, it would be inconvenient to some thousands of men and women who are just now cumbering the world to no purpose. It goes against the grain mightily to admit that a wild cat might ever become an angel; but if there is any obscure law tending to such a result, it is better to interfere with it as little as possible. If both moral and physical perfectibility are only a question of time, the fellow who sells his fiery potations close by that sweet mountain spring, and is never conscious of its perpetual rebuke, ought to have a margin, at least, of five million years.

There is a cleft in the mountain, about ten miles to the southwest of Santa Clara. That engineering was done by the Los Gatos. Entering this defile, the stage road winds along the mountain side for six or seven miles, and then turns to the right and goes down the mountain slope to Santa Cruz. But as long as there are any stage roads in sight, or signs of abrading wheels, you will find no trout. Turning to the left and following the ridge, at the height of about two thousand feet, a walk of three or four miles brings one to a point where civilization runs out with the disappearance of the last trail. That mountain lifting its dark crest so kingly into the clouds, is Loma Prieta, the highest crest of the Coast Range. On the north side of that intervening slope, and nearly a thousand feet higher, you will find the source of the Los Gatos. It is six miles away. There a great fountain bubbles out of the mountain side, and the stream, clear and strong, and singing for very joy, goes bounding on to the gorges below. The upper stream has never been defiled by sawdust; and no lout in shining boots ever went up to its head. It is best to go into camp here and take a fresh start the next morning. In the early dawn—before the sun glares on the land and sea—town and hamlet, valley and mountain, have a morning glory, which it were better not to miss. Looking oceanward, the fir and the redwood send up their spires of eternal green from all the valleys. At midnight, the full moon was flooding all the mountain top with light, and was apparently shining upon the still ocean, which had come quite to the base of the mountain. The fog had come in during the night, but hugged the earth so closely that every hillock appeared like an island resting on the calm, white sea. All night long the moon shone on this upper stratum, revealing with wonderful distinctness the tops of the tallest redwoods, while the trunks appeared to be submerged. It was not easy to dispel the illusion that one with a skiff might have paddled from wooded islet to another, treading a thousand intricate channels, drifting past the homes of strange peoples, whose lives were symbolized by this serene and silent sea. But the illusion would not hold water, when, at early dawn, a clumsy two-horse wagon went lumbering down the mountain and disappeared under this white stratum. When the sun came up, all the ragged and fleecy edges rolled in upon the center, and there was a silent seaward march, until at mid-day the fog banked up with perpendicular walls, about a dozen miles from the land. A little farther down the valley the trees were dripping with the moisture of this migratory ocean. But not a drop was collected on the glistening leaves of the madrono which gave us friendly shelter that night. It was a good place enough to sleep; but if one is to take an observation every half-hour during the night, he will have no difficulty in getting up at the call of the birds.

The first sound heard in the morning was the yelp of a miserable coyote. The intrusive rascal had pitched his key in advance of thrush, or lark, or robin. It was easy enough to silence him with a shotgun; but as the birds, also, would have been frightened into silence, this ill-favored vagabond was moderated by pitching two stones at him, with no other result than securing a lame shoulder for a week. The thing was entirely overdone; and if the fellow had any perception of the ridiculous, he went into his hole and laughed for the space of half an hour.

The altitude was too great for the home of robin and linnet. But the woodpeckers went screaming by, and the shy yellow-hammers flitted noiselessly from tree to tree; while, in the thicket, the cock quails were calling out the coveys for an early breakfast. Two deer had come down the mountain slope, and finally halted at half rifle-shot, looking stupidly at the camp-fire. If they understood the statute made in their behalf, they were perfectly safe. But Samson, who had stood for three minutes with one fore-leg raised in an intensely dramatic way, made a spring at last, and, without warrant of law, ran them down the canyon; and ten minutes later they were seen going up the opposite slope, but with many redundant antics, indicating contempt for the cur which had sought to worry them. Later in the day three or four more were seen, and one half-grown fawn was following the roe, the latter finally taking the wind and bounding off handsomely, while the fawn, less keen of scent, turned about and looked inquiringly, without any clear perception of danger. It was evident that so long as the fawn depends upon the mother for protection, it has not a very keen scent nor a quick apprehension of approaching danger. These are only perfected later, when the fawn is left to care for itself. The cub is very foolish; the young fox has no more of cunning than a common puppy; and a young ground-squirrel, in time of danger, rashly bobs his head out of the hole long before his venerable parents venture to take an observation. We might have had a smoking haunch of venison that morning, but it would have lacked that fine moral quality which the game law withheld. If you want to know the terrible power of temptation, breakfast on bacon when two deer are within rifle-shot.

It took not less than three hours to work through the interminable thickets, and to climb over the rocks, and gain a place for the first cast of a line. These mountain trout strike quick or not at all. There is a delicious, tingling sensation when the fellows jump from the eddies and swirls more than a foot out of water. You need not spit on your bait for luck, when the fish are breaking water for the hook, and the dark pools are alive with them; not very large, but with keen mountain appetites, having the brightest colors, hard of flesh, and gamy. Well, yes, here is where the fun comes in, after crawling for more than two miles through the brush, and over jagged rocks. Not the least of it is to observe that H— — has gone daft from over-excitement, and is throwing his fish into the tree-tops. What with the moon shining on his face last night, the deer coming down to tantalize him, and these mountain trout jumping wild for the hook, there is just as much lunacy as it is safe to encounter at this altitude.

The stream holds out well, and has not perceptibly diminished in a linear ascent of the mountain-side of nearly three miles. A never-failing reservoir, at an altitude of perhaps twenty-three hundred feet, creates the main branch; while lower down there is a constant augmentation from runnels, up some of which the trout find their way. It is best not to slight these little branches; for occasionally the water sinks, running underground for awhile, and then reappearing, so that a succession of pools is formed, which arrest the fish; and, having nothing to eat, they prey upon each other, until rarely more than two or three remain, and sometimes a solitary fish is left—he having ate up all his poor relations, and thus supplied their wants and his own. There is nothing very strange in this piscatory economy, after all. That bald-headed man, who lost his balance, and slid down a shelving rock nearly twenty feet into the pool, and went out on the other side, with a solitary fish dangling at his hook, and a most unearthly yell, is playing the same game in a business pool. There are more in it than can possibly succeed. One by one, he will eat up the others and become a millionaire. If a bigger fish in the pool eats him, it is only a slight variation of chances, which the commercial ethics of the times will just as heartily approve. You have made that pool desolate; but it is not necessary to yell so as to disturb the universe over a half-pound trout. If ever, O friend, you should have the luck to be drawn out of a pool thus, will there be no yelling in the subterranean caverns?

There is no heroism in jerking every fish out of the stream, just because they have keen mountain appetites. Moreover, as the rays of the sun become vertical, light is thrown into the pools and eddies, and the bites are languid and less frequent. An hour before sunset they will be as brisk as ever. But a hundred trout are enough for one morning, and too many, since no one is willing to carry them down the mountain. A year ago, an enthusiastic friend found the headwaters of the Butano, just over the ridge, toward the coast. Having cut his way out of the San Lorenzo Valley, making his own trail for seven miles or more, he cast in his hook where, he stoutly affirmed, no fisherman had ever preceded him. The falls in several places have formed deep basins in the soft, white sandstone. There this enthusiastic fisherman found his heaven for two hours, until night began to close in upon him. Did he go into a tree-top for the night, and pull his two hundred trout up after him? No; but he left them in a heap, and crept down the mountain at dusk, his pace quickened a little by the sight of a fresh bear-track. I do not think an honest bear, made fully acquainted with such sacrilegious conduct, would eat a man, or so much as smell of him.

All day long the perspective has been growing broader and richer, until these diminutive little fish, destined to be swallowed with a single snap of the jaws — even as they sought to snap the wriggling worm — have become a minor incident in the crowding events of the day. For an hour after dawn the only outlook was into the Santa Clara Valley. But the morning was cold; the thin gray smoke went up silently into the heavens from here and there a farm-house; across the valley a low column of mist clung to the foothills and rolled sullenly away. The rank vegetation of early spring, broken occasionally by the plowed fields, had all the abruptness of contrast seen in the patchwork of a bedquilt; and in the chill of the dawn was not a whit more pleasing to the eyes. But an hour later the sunlight filled all the valley; the harsher tints of the morning were melted into the more subdued glory of the spring, and one could fancy that the scent of almond blossoms came up the mountain, mingled with the grosser incense of the mold and tilth of many fields. Even the solitary stunted pine far up the mountain was dropping down its leafy *spicula*, like javelins cast aslant, and the last year's cones fell with a rattle, like hand grenades cast from some overhanging battlement. Life was crowding death even here, and the pine was freshening its foliage, as certain of spring time as the alder just shaking out its tassels by the river bank. Away to the southwest the Bay of Monterey, with its breadth of twenty miles, was reduced to a little patch of blue water; and wide off there was a faint trail of smoke along the horizon — the sign that a steamer was going down the coast for puncheons of wine and fleeces of wool.

The glass reveals the dome of a church at Santa Cruz, looking a little larger than a bird cage set down by the ocean. The famous picture on the ceiling of the old adobe church disappeared when the storms melted down the mud walls. If the perspective was faulty, the picture had a lively moral for bad Indians. But something better was found, not many years ago (so the village tradition runs), in one of the lofts in an old store-room near by. The *Padre* going up there with the village sign painter, to hunt for some half-forgotten thing, drew out of the lumber a lot of blurred and musty canvas, giving it to his friend. The latter hastened home and, unrolling his canvas, saw that upon one side there had once been a picture. But the pigment was now only powdered atoms, which a feather would sweep away. Oiling a new canvas, he laid it upon the back of the picture, and the oil striking through, the first process of restoration was safely accomplished. Then the surface of the picture was carefully cleaned. The sign painter quietly hung up his picture, satisfied that there was an infinite distance between it and a common daub. The *Padre* wanted the picture back after this sudden revelation of its wonderful beauty. But it never was transferred again to the old lumber room.

"What became of the *Padre*?"

"I think he went to heaven, where he found better pictures than were ever fished out of that old lumber room."

"And the sign painter?"

"Did you ever know a man who had a Murillo, or even thought he had one, who was in a hurry to leave this world?"

SHADOWS OF ST. HELENA.

WHETHER in the Russian River Valley, Napa, or the smaller valleys of the Clear Lake country, St. Helena is in such friendly proximity that all sense of isolation is destroyed. Looking toward the south from its shoulder, there was an endless succession of stubblefields and vineyards; the faint clatter of threshing machines could be heard; sacks of wheat stood bolt upright in the fields, like millers in convention. A train of cars, diminished by the long perspective, was creeping with serpentine undulations up the valley, and trailing a thin vapor against the sky. Farther south was the bay; white sails of little schooners, outlined by the glass, appeared to split the salt meadows open, as they crept toward the little town of Napa. St. Helena was grandly lifted up on that autumnal morning, and all the little mountains seemed to be rendering homage to the king.

There is no country under the sun where a vineyard is more picturesque than here. If there were an interminable perspective of green clothing and coloring all the hillsides, there would be no fitting border for the picture. But when there is not a fresh blade of grass by the wayside, and the tawny hills touch the yellow stubble-fields, we have a broad golden frame for some picture which ought to be worthy of it. And what more so than a sixty-acre vineyard, set within this mitred framework of mountains? The border is a very generous one, certainly—five or six miles of slope on either side, and this square of emerald in the centre. It is all worked in with true artistic effect, except those straight lines of vines, crossing at right angles. A poet or a painter, setting this vineyard, would have curved the lines, or secured an orderly disorder—enough, at least, to have destroyed the association with a schoolboy's rule and plummet.

Observe that the vines are not tied to clumsy, stiff stakes; nor are the leaves plucked off in part, to prevent mildew. The runners reach out and interlace, resting gently on the ground. The leaves droop a little in the hot sun, making a complete canopy for the clusters, the largest of which rest on the ground. How much more fitting this growing revelation—this discovery, step by step, of hidden clusters—than to see all this wealth at once, as one might do if the vines were trained bolt upright, and held in bondage by stakes!

Another notable effect is produced by the twenty or more varieties, differing in the shape of the leaf and in the color and flavor of the grape. The Tokay blushes by the side of the blackest Malvoisie. The Muscatel is pale where the Victoria has as much color as a ruddy English girl. The Muscats have a tinge of gold, in fine contrast with the Rose of Peru, whose regal purple deepens with every midday sun.

Three months hence, this border of gold will all be changed to the rank and riotous green of pastures quickened by the vernal rains—this square setting, as of emerald, stripped of every leaf and every cluster, but the bronzed vines still interlacing and toning the landscape into a mellow ripeness. A month later, the merciless pruning-knife has left only the black stub, a foot above the ground, and two or three "eyes" for the new wood. This amputated vineyard, with its limbs burning by the wayside, suggests enough of prosy realism to neutralize all the sentiment which it can inspire on a hot September day.

Will the juice of these grapes enrich the blood, and add any essential quality to the tone and fibre of a race which is giving so many signs of physical decadence? This conglomerate which you call society is hanging out a great many flags of distress. It babbles incoherently of perfectibility, and goes straightway to the bad. Are these reformers going to save the world, who, either through intemperance of speech or drink, must needs be moderated by a padlock put upon their mouths? Nor is it safe, just now, to calculate the results of this feminine gospel of vituperation. The back of the body politic may be the better for having a political fly blister laid on; and it might, perhaps, as well be done by feminine hands as any other. But there are some evils too deep for surface remedies. If, for instance, vineyards are going to curse the people, as my moralizing friend insists, then humanity hereabout is in a bad way. Why, a little generous wine ought to enrich the blood and inspire nobility of thought. If it does more than this—if it becomes a demon to drive men and hogs into the sea—then it is evident that both were on too low a plane of existence for any safe exaltation. But shall the vineyards be rooted up, for all this? It is better to drown the swine, and let the grapes still grow purple upon the hillsides.

Some day these mountains will be wreathed and festooned with vines. One may see this culture now climbing to their tops. Oh, my friend, with thin and impoverished blood! do not pinch this question up in the vise of your morality. No doubt there was a vineyard in Eden, and there were ripe clusters close by the fig-leaves. You cannot prove to me that sinless hands have not plucked the grapes, and that millions will not do it again. What we need is not a greater company of wailing prophets, but men who will reveal to us the higher and nobler use of things. If one could not live comfortably in this Vale of Paradise and ripen from year to year, opening his soul to all enriching influences, without an everlasting protest, there would be small chance for his comfort in any more etherealized place.

Looking northward, or from the back side of St. Helena, is Lake County, the centre of which can be reached by the daylight of a summer day from San Francisco. It is a wild, isolated and mountainous region, containing a harmless population, who are much addicted to salt pork, and needing all the more, perhaps, the medicinal and renovating qualities of the various thermal springs which abound. A Pike, with the wilderness at his back, and civilization advancing in front, is sometimes a ridiculous, and oftener a pitiable, specimen of humanity. When the schoolhouse overtakes him, there is a crisis in his affairs. He must elect to hustle half a score of frowzy-headed children into his covered wagon, hang a few pots and kettles at the rear, and plunge farther into the wilderness, or let civilization go past him, closing in upon all sides, and, in spite of impotent protests, narrowing perhaps his own horizon, but making it broader and brighter for his children. If the horizon is too bright, this blinking Pike will turn his back to the light, and make a break for Egypt. So long as there is bacon and hominy, and free territory, with a modicum of whisky within easy reach, you cannot summon this stolid, retreating animal to a better condition. Nature has made a botch of him, else he would now be running on four feet, instead of two. A border man, running away from civilization, who cannot bark and burrow like a coyote, nor climb a tree like a gorilla, is wrestling with his fate at a terrible disadvantage.

If you have never seen Clear Lake, do not babble about Como and Geneva. Here are eighty square miles of water, lifted fifteen hundred feet above the sea, and encompassed by mountains whose flaming forges were put out but yesterday—if a thousand years may be taken as one day. One may see Clear Lake from the top of St. Helena, twenty miles distant, on a bright day. We saw it first from Lukonoma—an intervening mountain, about fifteen hundred feet high—a ribbon of blue water, stretching away between the hills, with a solitary white sail, recognized only by bringing a tree in the range. There was the droning of the pines in the mountain-tops in the afternoon trade-wind; a broad valley opening to the south, which swallowed up two or three mountain streams, and then opened its ugly adobe lips for more; smaller valleys toward the north, encircled with tall firs, and the slumberous dome of Uncle Sam, lifting itself up grandly three or four thousand feet hard by the lake.

Along this Lukonoma ridge there is a well-defined Indian trail for miles. The Clear Lake Indians were accustomed to exchange visits with a tribe in the Lukonoma Valley, ten miles below. The tops of the highest mountain ridges were selected for trails, rather than the valley. The Indian does not like to be surprised, even by his friends. Along these ridges he could look off on either side, and a long way ahead. If not molested, he might drop down to the hot springs just at the base of the mountain, take a mud bath to make his joints a little more supple, and if he found an ant's nest to add to his dietary stores, so much the better. You need not overhaul the Indian's cookbook. He ate the ants alive. No shrimp-eater ought to quarrel with him on that score.

We shall have a nearer view of Lower Lake another day. It is better to have the first view of some old and famous city from the hill-tops. That revelation ripens into a picture which ever afterward we hasten to set over against the squalor and ugliness disclosed by a nearer view. One need not be wholly disgusted if in place of a trout, he has caught a mud-turtle from the lake which opened its sheen of waters to him first from the mountain summit.

The shadows had stretched nearly across the narrow valleys, when it occurred to us that, in climbing to the highest and baldest peak, the Indian trail had run out, and that the hot springs—the point of departure—were eight miles distant, and were shut out of view by an intervening spur. Either a short cut was to be made, trusting to luck to find a trail, or there was to be a night on the mountain. There were two intervening canyons to be crossed before there was any prospect of striking a trail. It is not pleasant to slide a horse on his haunches down into one of these chasms without knowing where one is to bring up. If the most obscure cattle trail can be found leading in, one may trust to the instincts of horse sense to find it, and also the one which will most certainly lead out on the other side. The tinkling of a cow-bell on the table-lands beyond was a welcome sound. The horses wound into the first canyon, and went out without much hesitation. The trail for the next, by good luck, had been found. But it was a suspicious circumstance that these ponies—accustomed to such defiles, and now heading for home—hesitated, snuffed, snorted and turned about. The rein was given to them, but, hungry as they were, they seemed disposed to turn back. The little Cayuse pony trembled, threw his ears forward, advanced and retreated, and blew out a column of vapor from each nostril as he kept up his aboriginal snort. Either two tired and hungry excursionists must make a night of it, shut in by a canyon in front and in the rear, or the second one must be crossed without delay.

A horse is generally willing to plant his feet where he sees a man do it in advance. But these horses were dragged into the chasm, sometimes dropping on their haunches, and at other times plowing along with the fore feet braced well ahead. Once at the bottom, a fresh cinch was taken with the greatest difficulty, as neither horse could be kept still for a second. A moment afterward the click of the pony's feet was heard, and the sparks thrown off by his shoes were distinct enough as he shot up the trail as though projected from a mortar. The old horse— stiff in the shoulders, and his legs like crowbars—was not a rod behind him.

"Did you see anything in that canyon?"

"No—yes. I saw the outline of a steer going down to drink."

"Nonsense! Do you think these tired horses, refusing first to come into the canyon, would have gone out on the other side as if Satan were after them, if they did not know that that particular steer had claws. If you had seen twenty mules break out of a yard and stampede when the foot of a cinnamon bear was thrown over, you would not blame these horses for blazing the trail with fire as they thundered up the rocks with the fresh scent of a live grizzly in their nostrils.

"Then, if you are willing to take the affidavits of these two horses as to the facts—and the jurat of eight steel-clad hoofs, striking fire on the rocks, was a very solemn one—you can settle the question in favor of the grizzly much more comfortably than he would have settled it for you. It is not necessary that one's scalp should be pulled over his eyes and his face set awry for life, in order to obtain a more convincing demonstration. I can refer you to a settler who has had these things done for him, whereat his satisfaction has in no whit increased."

An hour afterward two horses with drooping heads went into their stalls, and two jaded excursionists had each dropped into hot baths at Harbin's Springs. Nothing externally will neutralize the chill of a night ride among the mountains better than water which spouts from this hillside heated to 110 degrees. It is a notable caprice of Nature that, of three springs within the space of twenty feet, one is cold and has no mineral qualities; the other two are of about the same temperature, the waters of one strongly impregnated with iron and the other with sulphur. The waters of the two mineral springs combined are not only as hot as a strong man can bear, but they dissolve zinc bath-tubs, which was a satisfactory reason for the substitution of ugly wooden bathing-boxes. It is a pleasant nook, grandly encircled with mountains, with the wonderfully blue heavens by day, and lustrous stars by night.

Fifty or sixty moping invalids made up the assortment at the hotel. These taciturn and moody people did not wait for the angel to go down and trouble the waters, but each went in his own way and time, and troubled the waters mightily on his personal account. The fact may be assumed that the angel had been there in advance. For a thousand years, a great subterranean caldron had been heated, tempered and medicated, and its vapors had ascended as incense toward heaven.

This little sanitarium among the mountains, crowded with curious people—angular, petulant and capricious—was invested with a great peace and restfulness for brain-weary folk. When the sun went down, invalids, like children, went off to bed. There was nothing to do but to sleep through the long cool nights. All the conventionalities of a more artificial social life were reversed. The people who had fought Nature and common sense for years, and had been worsted in the conflict, came here to make their peace with her. They were up with the opening of the day. They drank medicated waters heroically; dropped into hot baths with a sensation akin to have fallen on the points of a million needles; plunged into pools, or were immersed with the vapors collected in close rooms. There were early breakfasts, when the boards were swept by invalids with ravenous appetites; dinners at midday, attended by the same hungry, silent, introspective people; supper, before sundown, when the same famishing people were eating away for dear life. A four-horse passenger wagon arrived just at nightfall, bringing the mail and an occasional guest. There was a glance at the newspapers, now and then a letter was read, and then night and a sweet stillness settled over this mountain dell. Time was of little consequence; people searched an old almanac for the day of the week or month; the sun rose above the crest of one mountain and went down behind another; there were the morning and evening shadows, the same flood of light in the valley at midday, the monotonous drone of the little rivulet in the canyon, and at long intervals the twitter of a solitary bird. Some sauntered along trails, counting the steps with a sort of mental vacuity; others tilted their chairs under porches, and slept with hats over their eyes. If a bustling, loud-voiced guest arrived, in a day or two he fell into the same peaceful and subdued ways. The repose of sky and mountain came down gently upon him, and a dreamy indolence shortened his steps and prolonged his afternoon naps.

There would have been an utter stagnation of life but for the advent of one of those characters who had been everywhere, seen everybody, and had become a sort of itinerating museum of odd conceits and grotesque incidents. There were many invalids who had separated themselves from business cares, only to brood over their infirmities. They wanted nothing so much as, in some way, to be led apart from their own morbid natures. The eccentric little man told his stories. They were not always fresh, nor always extremely witty. But, as the assortment never ran out, and the quality improved from day to day, the fact was alike creditable to his inventive powers and his benevolence. At first, the worst specimens of morbid anatomy listened from a distance, and muttered, "Foolish;" "Don't believe a word of it." The next day they hitched their chairs along a few feet nearer to this story-telling evangel. One could occasionally see that a crisis was coming; either these people must laugh, or be put on the list of hopeless incurables. Observing, on one occasion, a man on crutches who, after listening for a time with apparent contempt, suddenly withdrew and hobbled off around a turn of the narrow road, I ventured to ask him if stories were disagreeable to him.

"Oh, no, that is not it. You see I had not laughed in years. I was determined that old Hooker should not make me laugh, if I did not choose to. The fact is, I had either to holler or die. I wouldn't make a fool of myself, and so I went around the bend in the road, and turned off into the chaparral."

As this man dropped one crutch in a week from that time, and in ten days thereafter was walking with a cane, I have never doubted that he "hollered."

At nightfall generous wood fires glowed upon the hearth of the sitting room, and there was a more hopeful light in many faces. People lingered in the doorway, on the stairs, and leaned over the balustrade for one more story from the genial and eccentric man. A ripple of half-suppressed laughter went around the room, ran up the stair-way, and ended in gentle gurgles in the rooms with open doors at the end of the corridor. The man of anecdote and story had touched, with healing influences, maladies which no medicated waters could reach. He exorcised the demons so gently, that these brooding invalids hardly knew how they were rescued. New and marvelous virtues were thereafter found in the spring water; there was a softer sunlight in the dell; the man with the liver complaint became less sallow, and no longer talked spitefully about "Old Hooker"; and the woman who did not expect to live a week, no longer sent down petulant requests that the house might be still, but only wanted that last story repeated to her "just as he told it."

Once, as the twilight drew on, the face of Hooker seemed to glow with unwonted radiance, as he unfolded his plans for a sanitary retreat. His theory was, that civilization had culminated in mental disorders, and the world was running mad with excitements, which half-demented people were busy in fomenting. Of the sixty guests at the Springs, he estimated that, at one time, not more than seven per cent. were free from some sort of a delusion—the evidence of lunacy in its milder forms. If put into strait-jackets, or shut up in the wards of an hospital, or treated otherwise as if insane, they would become as mad as Bedlam. One delusion must be matched against another. Every man and woman must be treated as sane, and all that they did, or thought, or said, as the perfection of reason. The nonsense of clowns had cured more people than the wisdom of philosophers. The chemistry of Nature, the sunshine, the pure mountain air, and all the subtle combinations of thaumaturgic springs must be supplemented by every art which could beguile and lead people away from a miserable self-consciousness. A half-hour of sound sleep is sometimes the bridge over the gulf from death to life. He would not only make people sleep, but even laugh in their sleep. He would practice the highest arts of a sanitary magician. His patients should laugh by night and by day. They should forget themselves. The time would come when the best story-teller would be accounted the best physician.

On the evening before leaving the Springs, two hunters, in clay-colored clothes, deposited upon the porch each a deer and a string of mountain trout. Hooker, of blessed memory, after whispering confidentially the bill of fare for an early breakfast, went aside and talked in an undertone with the hunters, who soon afterward disappeared in the direction of the canyon we had crossed a few evenings before. The moon being nearly at full, there would be a good prospect for deer during the latter part of the night; but there was a possible hint of larger game, in the chuckling undertone of one of the hunters as he shouldered his rifle: "Fellers as wear them kind o' clothes don't know a bar when they see him."

In the early morning, the same hunters were warming their fingers by the wood fire in the sitting-room. Hooker was already up, and flitted about—now conferring with the hunters, and then with the steward. A game breakfast was already assured. Hooker whispered that the hunters had found the bear which sent the ponies flying out of the canyon. He had been taken alive, and we should have a parting look at him in advance of the other guests as we drove down the road. A Pike, astride of the corral fence, saluted Hooker as we were climbing to the top rail: "Glad you 'uns found old corn-cracker up the gulch. He was powerful weak when I turned him out. He's a good 'un."

One glance at his long, yellow tusks and bristling back was enough. There was a sudden snap of the whip, and the dust spun from the wheels as two horses shot down the road on a bright October morning. The little dell, with its thermal springs, its colony of invalids, Hooker, the incorrigible, and the "bear" in the corral, disappeared with a gentle benediction.

One may traverse a thousand miles of the Coast Range, and not find another mountain road which reveals, at every turn, so many striking views as the one of twenty miles from Harbin's to Calistoga. The road, for a considerable distance, follows the windings of a noisy and riotous little rivulet, which, heading on the easterly side of St. Helena, runs obstinately due north for several miles. The fringe of oaks and madronos were wonderfully fresh, as they stood half in sunlight and half in shadow, still dripping, here and there, with the moisture which had been condensed during the night. A delegation of robins had come down from higher latitudes, and were taking an early and cheery breakfast from the scarlet berries of the madrono. It needed but the flaming maple and falling chestnuts, with some prospect of "shell-barks," to round into perfect fullness these autumnal glories. But no one living east of the Hudson could raise such a wild and unearthly yell as broke from the Judge every time a cotton-tail rabbit darted across the road. The obstreperous woodpecker was awed into silence, and the more industrious ones dropped in amazement the acorns which they were tapping into the trunks of the trees, and flitted silently away.

"That," said the Judge, "is not half as loud as I heard Hooker yell six months ago."

"Then he was demented?"

"Yes; he was as mad as a March hare, and in a strait-jacket at that."

"That clears up one or two mysteries. But you might have made the revelation before."

"When are you going to start that hilarious institution which you and Hooker called a sanitarium?"

Just then, the summit of the mountain road had been gained, and the long perspective of the Napa Valley opened at the base of St. Helena, and melted away toward the south into the soft, dreamy atmosphere of an autumnal noonday.

THE HOUSE ON THE HILL.

A COUNTRY without grandmothers and old houses needs a great many balancing compensations. Everywhere one is confronted with staring new houses, which require an external ripening in the wind and sun for half a century. If the motherly wisdom of seventy-five years is lodged therein, it is something of recent importation. I have walked two miles to see an old lady, who not only bears this transplanting well, but is as fresh and winsome in thought as a girl of sixteen. If only there had been an old house, a stone fire-place—wide at the jambs—and a low, receding roof in the rear, with a bulging second story and oaken beams, nothing more would have been wanting.

When, therefore, it was whispered, one day, that there was an old house in the middle of a large lot on a hill, overlooking the Golden Gate, there was a strong and unaccountable desire to take possession of it immediately. But when the fact was stated that the house was ten years old, that there was moss upon the shingles, low ceilings within, and a low roof without, the destiny of that house was well nigh settled. The owner wanted money much more than old houses. In fact, a Californian who refuses to sell anything, except his wife, is only found after long intervals. The transfer of ownership was natural enough. It followed that one evening there was a dreamy consciousness that we were the owner of a small, rusty-looking cottage, set down in the middle of an acre lot, defined by dilapidated fences, and further ornamented by such stumps of trees as had been left after all the stray cattle of the neighborhood had browsed them at will. As incidents of the transfer, there was the Golden Gate, with the sun dropping into the ocean beyond; the purple hills; the sweep of the bay for fifteen miles, on which a white sail could be seen, here and there; and, later, the long rows of flickering street lamps, revealing the cleft avenues of the great city dipping toward the water on the opposite side of the bay.

Consider what an investment accompanies these muniments of title. It is not an acre lot and an old house merely, with several last year's birds' nests and a vagrant cat, but the ownership extends ninety-five millions of miles toward the zenith, and indefinitely toward the nadir. No one can, in miners' parlance, get an extension above or below. It is a square acre, bounded by heaven and hades.

If my neighbor builds an ugly house, why should I find fault with it, since it is the expression of his wants, and not of mine. If these are honestly expressed, he has compassed the main end of house-building. He may have produced something that nobody in the wide world will be suited with, or will ever want but himself. But if it is adapted to *his* wants, it is only in some remote and æsthetic way that his neighbors have anything to do with the matter. They may wish that he had not made it externally as ugly as original sin; that he had laid a heavy hand on the antics of architect and carpenter; that lightning would some day strike the "pilot-house," or some other excrescence which has been glued on to the top; and that a certain smart obtrusiveness were toned down a little to harmonize with a more correct taste. But one could not formulate these defects and send them to his neighbor without running a risk quite unwarranted by any good that might be effected.

Taking possession of an old house, its ugliness is to be redeemed, not rashly, but considerately, and in the spirit of gentleness. Its homeliness has been consecrated; its doors may have been the portals both of life and death. Possibly, some one has gone out whose memory of it in the ends of the earth will transform it into something of comeliness and beauty.

Investing an old house, the first process is to become thoroughly acquainted with it, and then, if it is to be enlarged, push it out from the center with such angles as will catch the sun, and will bring the best view within range from the windows. It will grow by expansions and accretions. You want a bed-room on the eastern side, because of the morning sun. By all means, put it there. The morning benediction which comes in at the window may temper one to better ways all the day.

No man will build a house to suit his inmost necessities, unless he proceeds independently of all modern rules of construction. Some of these are good enough, but they nearly all culminate in an ambitious externalism. The better class of dwellings erected seventy-five years ago contained broad staircases, spacious sleeping-rooms, and a living-room, where the whole family and the guests, withal, might gather at the fire-side. The house was an expression of hospitality. The host had room for friendships in his heart, and room at his hearthstone. The modern house, with its stiff angularities, narrow halls, and smart reception-rooms, expresses no idea of hospitality. It warns the stranger to deliver his message quickly, and be off. It is well adapted to small conventional hypocrisies, but you will never count the stars there by looking up the chimney.

One may search long to find the man who has not missed his aim in the matter of house-building. It is generally needful that two houses should be built as a sacrifice to sentiment, and then the third experiment may be reasonably successful. The owner will probably wander through the first two, seeking rest and finding none. His ideal dwelling is more remote than ever. There may be a wealth of gilt and stucco, and an excess of marble, which ought to be piled up in the cemetery for future use. But the house which receives one as into the very heaven—which is, from the beginning, invested with the ministries of rest, of hospitality, of peace, of that indefinable comfort which seems to converge all the goodness of the life that now is with the converging sunbeams—such a dwelling does not grow out of the first crude experiment. It will never be secured until one knows better what he really wants than an architect or carpenter can tell him.

"Did you bring the old house up to this ideal standard?" Just about as near as that pear tree, at the lower end of the garden, has been brought up to a perfect standard of fruiting. You perceive that where half of the top was cut away, and new scions inserted, the pears hung in groups and blushed in the autumnal sun. As you let one of them melt on your palate, turn to the other side of the tree, and note that, if ever a premium were offered for puckering, acrid fruit, these pears from the original stock ought to take it.

Now, if you graft your ideas on to another's, premising that his views were crude and primitive, the result will be somewhat mixed. We should say that the grafts put into that old house were tolerably satisfactory. But we counsel no friend to build over an old house, unless he owns a productive gold mine, and the bill of particulars at the end of his exploit is more interesting and gratifying to him than any modern novel.

There was, however, a shade of regret when it was announced that nothing more remained to be done. For three months there had been a series of gentle transitions, and an undercurrent of pleasurable excitement as a door appeared in a new place, a window opened here and there, stairways were cut, and old pieces pushed off and new took their places. It seemed as if these transitions ought to be always going on, and therefore the most natural thing in the world that the carpenters should always be cutting or hammering that house. They might grow old and another set take their places, but there would always be some room to enlarge, or some want growing out of the exigencies of a new day. Moreover, the first part taken in hand would in time decay or become antiquated, and why not associate builders and house together, since all the jars, wrenching of timbers, sawing and hammering had become musical, and seemed to be incorporated as the law of the house? Nothing but financial considerations prevented a contract for life with the builders, and the life-long luxury of changing an old house into a new one. There came a day at last of oppressive silence. Painters came down from their ladders; the carpenters packed up their tools and walked thoughtfully around, taking an honest view on all sides of a structure which had grown under their hands until, outwardly, there was not the slightest semblance of the old house which they took in hand some months before. There was a shade akin to sadness on the face of the master workman. Evidently the idea of ever leaving that house had overtaken him for the first time that day. He had grown with the house; or, at any rate, his children had been growing. Why should he not come back on the morrow, and plumb, hammer and saw; creeping up the ladder with every new day, and sliding down with every descending sun?

The loftiest house, and the most perfect, in the matter of architecture, I have ever seen, was that which a wood-chopper occupied with his family one winter in the forests of Santa Cruz County. It was the cavity of a redwood tree two hundred and forty feet in height. Fire had eaten away the trunk at the base, until a circular room had been formed, sixteen feet in diameter. At twenty feet or more from the ground was a knot-hole, which afforded egress for the smoke. With hammocks hung from pegs, and a few cooking utensils hung upon other pegs, that house lacked no essential thing. This woodman was in possession of a house which had been a thousand years in process of building. Perhaps on the very day it was finished he came along and entered it. How did all jack-knife and hand-saw architecture sink into insignificance in contrast with this house in the solitudes of the great forest! Moreover, the tenant fared like a prince; within thirty yards of his coniferous house a mountain stream went rushing past to the sea. In the swirls and eddies under the shelving rocks, if one could not land half a dozen trout within an hour, he deserved to go hungry as a penalty for his awkwardness. Now and then a deer came out into the openings, and, at no great distance, quail, rabbits and pigeons could be found. What did this man want more than Nature furnished him? He had a house with a "cupola" two hundred and forty feet high, and game at the cost of taking it.

It was a good omen, that the chimneys of the house on the hill had not been topped out more than a week, before two white doves alighted on them, glancing curiously down into the flues, and then toward the heavens. Nothing but the peace which they brought could have insured the serenity of that house against an untoward event which occurred a week afterward. Late one evening the expressman delivered a sack at the rear door, with a note from a friend in the city, stating that the writer, well knowing our liking for thoroughbred stock, had sent over one of the choicest game-chickens in San Francisco. The qualities of that bird were not overstated. Such a clean and delicately-shaped head! The long feathers on his neck shaded from black to green and gold. His spurs were as slender and sharp as lances; and his carriage was that of a prince, treading daintily the earth, as if it were not quite good enough for him. There was a world of poetry about that chicken, and he could also be made to serve some important uses. It is essential that every one dwelling on a hill, in the suburbs, should be notified of the dawn of a new day. Three Government fortifications in the bay let off as many heavy guns at daybreak; and, as the sound comes rolling in from seaward, the window casements rattle responsively. But these guns do not explode concurrently; frequently more than ten minutes intervene from the first report to the last one. There is ever a lingering uncertainty as to which is making a truthful report, or whether they are not all shooting wide of the mark. Then, there is a military school close by, which stirs up the youngsters with a reveille, a gong and a bell, at short intervals. With so many announcements, and none of them concurrent, there would still remain a painful uncertainty as to whether the day had dawned; but when that game bird lifted up his voice, and sounded his clarion notes high over the hill, the guns of Alcatraz and the roll of the drums over the way, there could be no doubt that the day was at the dawn.

For a week did this mettlesome bird lift up his voice above all the meaner roosters on the hill; but one morning there was an ominous silence about the precincts where he was quartered. The Alcatraz gun had been let off; but the more certain assurance of the new day had failed. Something had surely happened, for a neighbor was seen hurrying up the walk in the gray of the morning, red, puffy, and short of wind, at that unseasonable hour.

"Come with me, and take a look in my yard.... There, is that your blasted game chicken?"

"Why, yes—no—he was sent over as a present from a friend."

Just then the whole mischief was apparent; a great Cochin rooster was sneaking off toward the hedge, bloody and blind; two Houdans lay on their backs, jerking their feet convulsively—in short, that hen-yard had been swept as with the besom of destruction.

"Do you call that a poetical or sentimental bird, such as a Christian man ought to worship?"

"No, not exactly."

Just then that game chicken arched his beautiful neck and sent his clear notes high over the hill and into the very heavens. We hinted, in a mollifying way, that he had escaped over a fence ten feet high, but that blood would tell.

"Yes, I think it has told this morning. Never mind the damages; but I think you had better cut his wings," said our neighbor, already placated.

That bird was given away before the next sunset. But O! friend; by the guns of Alcatraz, and the white doves that alighted on the chimney-tops, emblems of war and peace, send us no more game chickens, to disturb the peace of the hill, or to finish the work of destruction begun on that unlucky morning.

From the hill one may look out of the Golden Gate, as through the tube of a telescope, and see all the watery waste and eternal scene-shifting beyond. When the dull, undulating hummocks look like a drove of camels in the desert, you may be sure that the newly-married couple just embarking on the outward-bound steamer, on a bridal tour to Los Angeles or the Hawaiian Islands, will cease their caroling and chirping within an hour. Half an hour after sunset, if the atmosphere is clear, one may see the wide-off light of the Farallones; the nearer lights of Point Bonita and Alcatraz, almost in line, dwarfed to mere fire-flies now; but when the Gate has lost the glow of its burnished gold, these great sea-lamps, hung over this royal avenue, tell an honest home story for the battered ships low down on the horizon.

The little tugs which round under the quarters of the great wheat ships and rush them out to sea, know how to overcome the inertia of the great hulks. They tug spitefully, but the ship has to move, and you see the white sails already beginning to fall down from the yards, for the work where the blue water begins. It may be a grotesque association, but have you never seen a small woman, with a wonderful concentration of energy, tug her great lazy hulk of a husband out into the broad field of earnest endeavor in much the same way? Once there, his inertia overcome, the feminine tow-line cast off, he did brave and honest work, making the race quite abreast of average men. But the woman, who tugged him from his lazy anchorage out into a good offing, did as much for that man as he ever did for himself. Nothing more fortunate can happen to a great many men than that they be towed out to sea early. And in not a few instances, nothing more unfortunate could happen than that they should ever return. This last remark would have been softened a little, had it not been repeated with emphasis by a tender-hearted woman.

Just after a winter rain, there are occasionally realistic views of the great city in the foreground, which are so ugly that one never forgets them. The hills are brought nigh; all the houses seem to rise out of the desert, and along the water front the spars of shipping look like a forest which has been blasted by some devouring flame. It is certain that these forests will never sprout again; and there is such a dead look that, were it not for the little tugs going back and forth, one might imagine that all men had hastened away, and left the city to silence and the desert. But after nightfall the thousand lamps glorify the city; the blackened forest along the water front has faded out; and a mild sort of charity steals over one, suggesting that, after all, it is a goodly city set upon a hill, and that its peculiar beauty is not alone in appearing to the best advantage by gaslight. The background of hills is more angular and jerky than ever before, because all the softening effect has been taken out of the atmosphere. There is no distance, no dreamy haze to spread like a gossamer veil over these hard outlines. Nature is wonderfully honest and self-revealing. Evidently these hills were never finished. They lack all the rounded beauty, all the gentle curves and slopes, and all the fine touches of a perfected work. They look as if, when in a plastic state, they had been set by the jerk of an earthquake. Who knows but another jerk might take these kinks out and tone down all these stiff angles, and otherwise put on the finishing touches? If it must be done in this way, let the softening undulations be as gentle as possible. It is very inconvenient to get up in the morning and find that the chimney-top is either on the garden walk, or that it has been turned three-quarters round, in the very wantonness and devilment of Nature.

Some day there will be a closer recognized relation between landscape gardening and landscape painting. If the work is done badly in either department, it will make little difference whether an acre of canvas is hung upon the wall, or whether lines have been badly drawn and colors crudely laid on to an acre of earth. The style of trimming trees so that they are a libel on Nature, and the geometrical diagrams worked up in a garden, can hardly be referred to any very high standard of art. But if my neighbor is delighted with trees representing spindles, ramrods, paint brushes, cylinders, cones, and what not, I would no more quarrel with him than with the man who is under the pleasing delusion that he is an artist, because, in a more remote way, he has been traducing Nature with certain grotesque figures laid on to canvas.

A hedge will bear cutting into line, because it is to be treated as nothing more than the frame of the landscape to be worked up. The former may be as stiff and artificial in its way, as a gilt or mahogany frame, and do no violence to good taste; if it hides an ugly fence, a point has been gained. One cannot expect much diversity of surface on a single acre. A large lawn will give the effect of greater flatness. If you find the hired gardener, bred in some noted school in Europe, setting out trees in straight lines, exhort him to penitence at once. If he remain obdurate, cut the trees down with your little hatchet and pitch them over the fence, but keep your temper as sweet as a June morning. He will see by that time that you have ideas to be respected. Grouping the trees, on the lawn and elsewhere, neutralizes, in part, the effect of a flat surface; it is better than the poor apology of a little hillock, which suggests an ant's nest, or that a coyote may be burrowing in that vicinity. Something may be done in the way of massing colors with annuals to produce good effects. But ribbon gardening, according to the patterns laid down by florists, has no nearer relation to art in landscape gardening than crochet work has to landscape painting. It is a fantastic trick, which may very well please rural clowns, but is in some sort an offense to good taste.

Neither is it necessary that all the trees and shrubs which a florist has for sale should be admitted to the private garden. More than one-half of them have no merit; they neither set off the grounds, nor have any peculiarity worth a moment's attention. They figure in the florist's list under very attractive names, but if taken home they will probably prove but scrubby little bushes, fit only to be dedicated to the rubbish-heap and the annual bon-fire in the Spring. A plant or a shrub which gives no pleasure either in its form or the color of its flower, and has no suggestive associations, may do well enough for a botanical garden. Many of us may like occasionally to look at a hippopotamus or an elephant in the menagerie, or at the zoological gardens, but we don't want these specimens brought home to our private grounds. Some of the *sequoia gigantea* family do very well in the forest. Once in a lifetime we can afford to make a journey to look at them. But why undertake to bring home one of these vegetable elephants as a specimen, when we know that it will require a thousand years for its growth, and that most of us will come a little short of that measure of time? Some trees may be planted for posterity, and others may be safely left to take their chances. If any one wishes to contemplate upon his grounds a shrub of the future dimensions of one of the Calaveras group, let him plant it at once. Most of the vegetable monsters went out with the ichthyosaurus, and as for the few that remain, they will yet be an affront to the pigmies who are swarming on the earth.

"Why did we plant cherry trees along the rear fence?" To make friends with the birds and the children. You can get more songs from the birds, and more of song and glee from the children, on a small investment in cherry trees than in any other way. Those last year's birds' nests tell the story. The robin, thrush, oriole and linnet will come early and stay late. Groups of children will come in the front way, and will never be so happy as when invited to go down the rear garden walk, unless in the supremest moments when they step from your shoulders into the trees, and never come back until they have closed their fingers on the last cherry. The man who is not satisfied to divide all his cherries with the birds and the children is a curmudgeon; notably so is he who plants cherry trees in front of his lot, and gets into a white heat of rage because boys of average Sunday school antecedents could not resist the temptation to borrow the fruit. Besides, the eclectic judgment of children, the sparrow, the yellow-jacket and the honey-bee will always tell you where the best nectarines and plums may be found.

It is well to reserve a nook for little experiments in horticulture or floriculture which one wishes to make. A great many theories may be brought home and decently buried, or be made to sprout in such a corner. The larger the spaces, the more one will be tempted to use the spade at odd hours; and none of us has yet found out all the remedial qualities of dry earth freshly turned over day after day. A hard day's work, taxing brain more than hands, brings on a degree of nervous irritability. There is a dry electrical atmosphere; the attrition of trade winds and sand half the year; and the rushing to and fro of busy and excited men, charged as full of electricity as they can hold, and bent upon charging everybody else, so that at nightfall the sparks will snap at the finger-ends, and the air will crackle like a brush-heap just set on fire. Now, the earth is a very good conductor. It is better to let this surplus electricity run down the fingers on to the spade, and along its shining steel blade into the ground, than to blow up your best friend. An hour of honest battle with the weeds is better than any domestic thunder storm. By that time the sun will have dropped down into the ocean, just beyond the Golden Gate, glorifying garden and hill-top, and setting, for a moment, its lamp of flame in the western windows. Every plant and shrub will have some part in a subtile and soothing ministry; and then, if ever, it will occur to you that this is a mellow old world after all.

THE GARDEN ON THE HILL.

It was a plausible theory, and given out in a demure and confiding way by a feminine oracle, that honeysuckle cuttings should each be inserted in a potato, and so planted. As the scion had no root and needed moisture, it would be supplied by the potato. It seemed the very thing to do. The wonder was that so simple an expedient had not been suggested before. That theory was honestly tested, and it has since been laid on the top shelf with a great many other feminine theories about floriculture. Twenty honeysuckle scions were each planted with one end in an enormous red potato. Never did one of those honeysuckles grow; but there sprang up such a growth of potatoes as never had been seen on the hill. They were under the doorstep, under the foundation of the house; they shot up everywhere. Was that the last of the misadventure? By no manner of means. In the very porch of the church that daughter of Eve inquired slily, "How are your honeysuckles?" And then she glided in as if she had done nothing for which she needed forgiveness.

Certain grafting experiments came out a shade better. But every graft put in on the south side of a tree died, while those on the north side nearly all lived. These were protected by some degree of shade, while the hot sun melted the wax on the south side, which ran down in liquid streams of resin and poisoned the bark around the cleft. All this might have been known in advance. But a little modicum of knowledge learned by costly experience will stick to one through life, while that which costs nothing is rarely laid up as worth having. It ought to be known, also, that there is no better plan of grafting a tree than that which our ancestors followed a hundred years ago, when, with a little moist clay and top-tow, every scion inserted lived. Then the cider mill was an orthodox institution in every neighborhood. It is not worth your while to dissent from that proposition, when you have probably played truant from a summer school to ride around on the sweep of a cider mill, and suck the new cider through a straw, being stung the meanwhile occasionally by a "yellow-jacket." Even now a cider mill by the roadside, with the sour pomace scattered about, is a humanizing institution. It will send you back to the old orchard, the great branching elm, and the wide-spreading roof slanting down in the rear, quicker than any other sign or symbol to be found along the dusty way of middle life. For one hour's ride on that sweep, and a nibble at the spice-apples sliding down the hopper, one might still be consoled for the dreadful frown of the school mistress, and for that feminine refinement on purgatorial cruelty which compelled the truant to stand for an hour on one leg, and to hold out a bible at arm's length in his dexter hand. An acidulated school mistress, who had been losing her sweetness for forty years, never was a desirable object to meet, after having tasted the sweets on a summer day at a cider mill. The hornets were well enough in their way, but the sting of that school mistress was not.

Note, too, that this grafting process reaches over beyond your apple trees. The best races, or sub-divisions of people, come of the best stocks which are continually grafted on. Your blue blood is mixed with more not so blue, or the stock runs out. Down at the root of those apple trees yonder you may find traces of the woolly aphis. It is a sign that the constitution of such trees has been weakened. Digging down you remove the aphis, put fresh soil around the tree, scrape the rusty trunk, cut off the top, and put in two or three grafts from a stock that has vitality; and very soon this rejuvenated tree, bending under its weight of fruit in early Autumn, is something of which no amateur horticulturist need be ashamed. A thoroughbred people will impress language, law, and custom, as none other can upon the world. It is not isolation which secures this result, but the taking of many stocks upon the original trunk. If pulmonary New England is to be physically resuscitated, it will not come of boasting of revolutionary sires, but rather because Germans, Irish, Danes and Swedes are thronging all the avenues of her busy life.

The transition from grafting to budding is natural enough. Those twenty white stakes stand as so many monuments of another horticultural disaster. On a September day, twenty buds, so rare that the original stock could not be bought at any price, had been deftly slipped into as many "suckers," which had come out from the roots of as many rose bushes. The next Spring they were set and staked, and each was about as precious as the right eye of any amateur horticulturist. The small buds had developed into branches a foot long; great double peerless roses had been hanging pendent from the original stocks—roses with regal names and titles. There would have been twenty glorified specimens of floriculture to-day, but for that foreign gardener who had been "educated in the best schools in Europe," who knew everything, and could not be told anything. Roses must be cut in to make new wood. Before night he had clipped those twenty standards each below the bud, and had taken himself off with his diabolical shears, his insufferable conceit, and his rustic innocence. He never came back to look at the work of his hands, nor to hear the wish (mildly expressed) that a pair of shears might be invented which would shorten the stature of that gardener at least a foot. There was a special aggravation of the case, because we had been nursing a theory for years, that by splitting two rose-germs of different kinds, and putting the odd halves together, if growth could then be induced, there would be a hybrid rose—either the color of the one would be distinct on one side, and the other on the opposite side, or the rose would be mottled, having red and white spots on each leaf. This Siamese bud had started finely. Bad luck to the gardener's shears which had abbreviated that experiment and enveloped the vexed question again in darkness. But here is a bed of mottled pinks, and these could have all been the result of crosses. It may be that the humming birds, going from one blossom to another, have mixed the pollen, or some hidden law may be active which cannot be traced. Note, too, that besides this promiscuous fleck of red and white, in not a few instances a single flower will have the red on one-half and the white on the other. The florists call this sporting. The same class of facts may be observed in the double petunias, all of which are hybrids, or nearly so—a purple, white, and red leaf being found in a single flower. There are apples, too (or there were twenty years ago), one-half of which were sour and the other half sweet. The qualities were not interblended, and even the colors were separate.

It was a pretty conceit, and mollifying withal, that a feminine florist connected with pansies: "When you go past them they will turn their heads toward you, greeting you so lovingly." That little myth might be strung on the same string with the buttercup, which only reflects its golden hue upon the chins of those who love June butter.

That alfalfa experiment is only admitted by special grace under the head of floriculture, although the lucerne has no lack of handsome blossoms. A little seed was sprinkled on the ground after the spring rains and forgotten. When the winter rains came again, that alfalfa reached out for both the zenith and nadir. Three times a year it is cut to keep it from falling down. The details are suppressed here, with only an intimation that they are sufficient for several agricultural addresses. If that man is a benefactor who has made two blades of grass grow in the place of one, what is he who has made alfalfa shoot up at the rate of seven tons to the acre, in the place of miserable sorrel-top? But there was a discount upon that experiment. The alfalfa drew to it all the gophers in the neighborhood. They mined and countermined, until the whole area had been honeycombed. They multiplied by scores and hundreds. These rodents drew together all the vagrant cats in the neighborhood, which made this corner of the garden a common hunting ground. Here upon this small area was a crop of alfalfa, a crop of gophers—which no man has numbered to this day—and a crop of cats, as fiercely predatory and as unrelenting in a skirmish as were ever put in battle array. But somehow this experiment has not been satisfactory. It has branched out in too many ways. Two empty arnica bottles suggest the muscular strains which came from moderating those cats with an occasional volley of rocks. And at this writing, half a dozen felines are on the fence looking solemnly down at the sapping and mining which is going on below.

There are no birds in this region which domesticate so readily as the linnets, and which improve more on an intimate acquaintance. They are not so obstreperous as the wren, nor so shy as the lark and the robin. The latter is a migratory bird, coming down to this latitude only in the Winter, and going north for a nesting in the Spring. A single robin has lived in the garden all Winter, becoming nearly as tame as a chicken, following the man with the spading-fork, and snapping up the worms in a sharp competition with his cousin, the brown thrush. The former, in place of any song, has a lonesome and fugitive call, as though waiting for his mate. He is probably a bachelor, who has not yet set up an establishment of his own. A little girl, having gravely considered the case, suggests that he ought to send a letter inviting a mate to come. O, my little friend! oral communication is much more interesting; at least, it was so in our time. Neither was it considered cowardice if the heart came up into the throat.

The linnets are model birds in their domestic life. A pair built a nest last year under the porch, and, having brought up one family of four and dismissed them, the pair furbished up the nest again and brought up a family of four more the same season. They have held secret conferences over the nest recently, and it evidently falls in with their views of domestic economy to use it again. It is possible that they appreciated a little device which we had to adopt for their safety. As the nest was at the extremity of a festoon of vines, there was nothing to hinder the house-cat from going up and feasting on callow birds. An odd lot of trout hooks, fastened to the lower vines, operated as a powerful non-conductor.

Some years ago, a pair of linnets having made their nest in the porch of another house, everything went well until the young had just appeared; then the mother disappeared one night, and the displaced vines in the morning told the whole story. Four orphan birds appealed to the sympathies of the young folk. The nest was taken into the house, the birds carefully covered with cotton, and every effort was made to save them. They would eat nothing, and, as a last resort, the nest was replaced in the vines. The father came back soon, talked with his children, brooded them, fed them day after day, brought them up to maturity, and turned out as prosperous a family of young linnets as there was in that neighborhood. Mr. Linnet can have the most positive certificate of rare domestic virtues. There is the slight drawback that he paints, does all the singing, and is rather vain; while Mrs. Linnet is a plain, unassuming bird, always clad in gray, and is not up in music. All through the realm of ornithology the male bird has the brightest colors and does the singing. But analogy is all at fault when you come to men and women. Who puts on all the bright colors here, paints, and carols upon the topmost bough of the domestic tree? By what law has this order been reversed? And yet the sum of your political economy is, that a woman who can dress more, use pigments more cunningly, and talk faster, and sing better than a man, shall not vote! Is that the way to set up your ideal republic?

One may learn secrets of ornithology in the garden which the books will not yield up. That boy coming up the rear garden walk, who has swung himself into a pear tree to look into the nest of a finch, has done the same thing consecutively on a dozen mornings. He will be able to tell just how many days are required for incubation, and how many days intervene before the birds are full-fledged. I should have had more hope for him as a future ornithologist, had not the young heathen asked for the eggs to put upon his string. There is not such a great difference, after all, between an Apache with a string of scalps at his belt, and a school boy with his string of birds' eggs. If it were not for that infernal cruelty which has been inbred by false teaching, or no teaching, our relations with all the lower forms of life would be intimate and confidential, instead of suspicious and oftentimes revolting. One can match the worst specimens of cannibalism by pointing out strings of larks hung up by their bills any day in the market. I know of no cannibal who ever became ferocious enough to eat singing birds, or to find pleasure in killing them.

There are two or three notes in the song of the lark which are not surpassed in sweetness by any of the oriole or finch family. If one will take a dash into the country some bright morning, on horseback, and note how this joyous bird goes before him, alighting on the fence and calling down a benediction from the heavens, either he will come back filled with gladness, or his liver trouble has got the best of him. All the song birds of much note in this State may be assigned to the three families of thrushes, orioles and finches. In the first of these we have the robin; in the second, the lark; and in the third, the linnet. The sub-families will reach nearly a hundred, and there is not one of them which will not pay in songs and in the destruction of insects for all the mischief he does. Now, a bird that pays his bills in advance, has a right to protection. Observe, too, how soon they recognize any attempt to establish friendly relations with them. Last year a finch had her feet entangled by a string with which she had lined her nest. A little help rendered to set her free, made her an intimate friend, and a shallow pan of water in the grass drew daily dividends of fresh songs. A box with a few holes in it, set on a post, will not remain empty a year; either the blue-birds or the martins will take possession of it.

A garden ought to be planned as much for the birds as for lawns and flowers. The hedges will afford hiding-places for timid birds, and shade on hot days. The tall trees will furnish perches when they want to sing; and a well-fed bird, that has no family trouble on hand, wants to sing nearly all his leisure time. As for the cherries and small fruits, the birds are only gentle communists. If we cannot tolerate a division made with all the inspiration of song, and which leaves us at least one side of the cherry, how are we to tolerate that division predicted by some of the labor prophets, if made with the music of paving-stones and much fragile crockery?

One cannot go far into the woods in any direction without observing what a protest all the birds utter at first. There are harsh screams, sharp notes of warning, and general scolding. Now, every bird has a great deal of curiosity to take a look at strangers. For a time they flit about in the tall tree-tops, and afterward begin to hop down to lower limbs, and, gradually descending, come to the ground, or on to low bushes. By remaining quiet an hour or two, a dozen or more will circle around within a few feet, turning their heads on one side occasionally, and quizzing in a saucy, merry way. In a little while one may be on intimate terms with the very birds which protested so loudly at his coming. They will tell him a great many secrets. The leaves of his book on ornithology may be a quarter of a mile square, but what can not be read on one day may be read on some other. Even an owl burrowing with a ground-squirrel, and both agreeing very well as tenants in common with a rattlesnake, may suggest questions of affinity and community which it might be inconvenient to answer at once. If you prefer to have some readings in a book of nature, you can turn down a leaf and go back the next day with the certainty that no one has lugged off the volume. And if your finger-mark is a tree 250 feet high, there will be no great difficulty in finding the place.

But a garden of a single acre can only be at most, a diamond edition of nature. A great deal must be left out. The owl, as a singing-bird, is not wanted; and, although tadpoles may be raised in the little fish-pond, it is not expected that the hippopotamus will come there to wallow. The birds must of necessity be few and select. If the lark sometimes sings at sunrise on the lower fence, and the thrush and the linnet bid you good morning out of the nearest tree-tops, you will not fail to respond, unless on that particular morning when you especially need an extract of dandelion; and that will generally happen when the golden blossoms can be found along the way-side. It might be well, also, to leave a little nook for sage and worm-wood. They are not only handsome plants in their way, but the average wisdom of any grandmother will unfold their remedial properties.

There are seven well-defined species of humming-birds to be found in this State, and two or three more not described, except in the unpublished notes of Grayson. None of these birds are singers; the best they can do is to make a noise like the turning of a small ratchet-wheel. But somehow, this ungenial, obstreperous little bird, darting in a saucy way close to one's ears, and then, balancing over a flower, never ceases to excite interest. He might have dropped out of Paradise, if it were not for his temper, which lacks any heavenly quality, and for his song, which would soon raise a mutiny above or below. He is a half unreal bird; and we do not know what soul in a transition state may be lodged in his little body. There are a great many souls small enough to occupy it. Now, the house-cat had been taught, after a long time, to respect birds, and that to look longingly at a humming-bird was something akin to sacrilege. But original sin, or instinct, was always ready to break out at the sight of a humming-bird. One evening she trotted down the garden walk with head up and a diminutive bird in her mouth. It took a lively turn of three times or more around that acre lot to overhaul that cat; nor was it done until the pursuer was thoroughly red in the face and blown, having just strength enough left to gripe her by the throat and make her let go. It was the poorest job of bird-philanthropy ever done in that garden. There was nothing to reward a merciful man but a humming miller, of just the size and finish, from bill to wings, of a humming-bird, but only an ugly bug as to his posterior half—a creature with his head and wings over in the realms of ornithology, and the rest of his ugly body still in the field of entomology. The quality of mercy is strained which undertakes to protect any such half-formed work of creation. When, therefore, a few evenings afterward, a *shrike*, or butcher-bird, came into the garden, devoured half a dozen of these bogus humming-birds, and hung up as many more on the thorns of a honey-locust, that circumstance suggested no doubt about the eternal fitness of things.

The quail is easily domesticated in any garden, and, if protected, will become as tame as the chickens. I have more than once seen them run where a hen was scratching, and pick up whatever could be found. Some years ago, while mowing the grass around the edges of another garden, a nest was discovered containing a dozen hen's eggs and *seventeen* quail's eggs. The village *savants* never did fairly settle the questions raised about that nest. Did the hen have the prior right, first choosing the place and making the nest? or did the quail pre-empt, and was the hen an unlawful squatter? Did they lay on alternate days, or concurrently as to time? And how did the eggs get that arrangement by which all the crevices were filled with the smaller ones? And which did the incubating? The quail could not cover the nest. But nearly all the eggs of both sorts were ultimately hatched. It had been settled before that time, by our system of patriarchial jurisprudence, that the issue followed the condition of the mother. The chicks respected that principle, since so rudely questioned, and each followed its mother, so that substantial justice was done, and the heavens did not fall.

No garden is well stocked without a pair or two of toads. They will learn to distinguish your foot-steps from those of a stranger, as they come out at twilight. The toad is a philosopher, and is the most self-contained of all living things. He meditates all day in the shade, and takes his dinner promptly at twilight. That dinner may require a thousand insects. The dart of his tongue is never made amiss. If you cannot cultivate him for his beauty—and there may be a doubt on that score—you can tolerate him for his honest work. There is some cant about the ugliness of the toad that you would not respect when you have taught a pair to come out of their hiding places at your call, have given them pet names, and have seen them slay the remorseless mosquito. If you step on one after nightfall, it will be useless to objurgate. You cannot provoke him to talk back.

Consider what an advantage the toad has in another respect. He not only hibernates a part of the year, and thus saves his board-bills, but he has been known to suspend active life for a quarter of a century or more; as when, getting into a hollow tree, the orifice has been filled up, or he has been wedged in the cleft of a rock. But when restored, he resumes life with no inconvenience to his digestion. What might be gained if one only had the vitality of this batrachian! You have been overtaken by a stupidly dull era, or are disgusted with life. What an advantage to call on some friend to pack you away in ice, and to thaw you out only when the next quarter-century bell rings! Since we cannot go safely over this bridge with the batrachian, it is not well to put such a discount on his ugliness, nor is it well to be too exclamatory, if you tread on him in the twilight.

The garden is the place to test a great many pretty theories. And what if some of them fail? Is not the sum of our knowledge derived from failures, greater than all we have ever gained by successes? A feminine oracle, not content with her honeysuckle theory, had said: "You must not pull up a plant nor a vine that springs up spontaneously. Let it grow. There is luck in it." When, therefore, a melon-vine made its appearance quite in the wrong place, it was spared through the wisdom of that oracle. It went sprawling over the ground, choking more delicate plants, and rioting day by day in the warm sun and the rich loam underneath. Nearly all its blossoms fell off without fruitage. One melon took up all the life of the vine, and grew wonderfully. There had been tape-line measurements without number. When it gave out a satisfactory sound by snapping it with thumb and finger, and the nearest tendril had dried up, it was held to be fully ripe. It was *very* ripe. A gopher had mined under that melon, and, not content with eating out the entire pulp, had, in the very wantonness of his deviltry, tamped the shell full of dirt! Where was the luck in this spontaneous growth? Nor did the matter end here. Sometime thereafter the following note, written in a feminine hand, was found pinned to that shell:

"Garden on the Hill, August 20, 187—.

"Mr. B——: *Dear Sir*—Since you have had the benefit of my discovery of the new method of planting honeysuckles inserted in potatoes, and you have also tested my theory of the luck there is in melon-vines of spontaneous growth, it has occurred to me that you would fully appreciate my skill and attainments. Now, I expect to be a candidate for the Chair of Horticulture and Floriculture in the University. I must have strong recommendations. Will you be kind enough to furnish me a certificate in which full justice is done to my attainments? My success may hinge on that certificate. Make it as strong as you can with a good conscience.

AGRAPINA.

P. S.—I forgot to tell you that if you had pinched out the eyes of the tubers in that first experiment, while you would have had less potatoes, you might not have had any more honeysuckles."

A.

That certificate was fully prepared. If we know anything about our mother tongue, the qualifications of the applicant were fully set out. Singularly enough, she has never applied in person for the document.

The almond tree is worthy of a place in every garden, even if it never fruits. The pale blush of its blossoms is the herald of Spring. In the warm days of February it puts on a pink dress, and is glorified. The bees come out, lured evidently by the scent of its flowers; but they flit about in a fugitive way, as if not satisfied with what they had found. There are small resources of honey in the almond blossoms; so much might be learned from the spiteful way in which the humming-birds darted off after sounding a little with their long bills. Something like one almond came to maturity for every thousand buds which unfolded in the early Spring. Two or three hundred "paper shells" clung to the tree hard by the library door, in the late Autumn. Whatever had been the fortune of other almond growers, here was a crop by an amateur. It was of no consequence that there had been a great discrepancy between flowers and fruit. Precious things are never abundant. No, by no manner of means, were these almonds to grace any Thanksgiving table. Let thanks be given for the brown shells clinging to the tree, and for whatever of internal good this outwardness might suggest. And not least, for the humming-bird's nest on the end of a pendent limb, so like a warty excrescence of the tree as not to be observed by careless eyes—and for that mutual confidence when curly-headed children were lifted up, and birds and children communed face to face, chirruped, and were glad.

"What became of the almonds?" There was a case of misplaced confidence. It was well enough that the finch, the linnet, the chat and the sparrow, had plucked the cherries, sampled the plums, and had taken kindly to the mellow side of the pears. December had come. Only here and there a fugitive gross-beak flitted about—a bird with a wonderful capacity for mellow song, but silent, as if never a note had gone out of his capacious throat and chubby bill. Perhaps they could be induced to sing in midwinter if confidence could be established. Half a dozen almonds were laid on the walk, which a pair of gross-beaks "shucked" with wonderful facility. That stout, short beak is fitted for a nut eater. Half an hour afterward there were twenty gross-beaks on that almond tree; and forty minutes later, they had stored every almond in their crops, cutting away the shells as deftly as one could do with a sharp knife. So tame and bold were they that one could have nearly reached them with his hand. Not a note was given in return, nothing but a twitter, as much as to say, "This is a royal dinner; there were just enough nuts to go round." And then they went off silently into the blue sky.

The first man, being historically and traditionally perfect, had a garden as his noblest allotment. The farther the race drifts away from the cultivation of the soil, the nearer it gets to barbarism. The Apache is not a good horticulturist, and therefore there is no gentleness in his blood. Teach him to love and cultivate a garden, and he is no longer a savage. The best thought and the best inspiration may come to one when all the gentler ministries of his garden wait upon him—when the soul of things is concurrent with his own, and bee and almond blossom, the rose, and the smallest song-sparrow in the tree-top, are revelators and instructors.

THE HOMESTEAD BY THE SEA.

THE sighing and respiration of the great sea to-day was wonderfully soothing, until there was a series of dull explosions, like the percussion of far-off gunnery. One may hear these sounds on a still midsummer day, or at midnight, when the sea is pulsing and breaking along the shore line. It required two hours to find out the secret. Along these chalk cliffs there are great caverns, wind and wave worn. Standing near the mouth of one of them, a "boomer" came surging along, and placed its watery seal over the mouth, driving and pressing the atmosphere before it. When the seal was broken there was an explosion like a gun seaward. The turn of the tide is frequently marked by a series of these boomers, and then there is a suggestion of a park of artillery under the cliffs, and the long roll is beaten along the shore. All discoveries are simple enough when once the secret has been found out. How many men walk along the edge of a discovery all their lives, and never quite enter into the promised land! Some blundering successor stumbles into the fruition of the great secret. There are men within bow-shot of prizes as magnificent as ever crowned human research; but they will go no farther. Columbus rested at the Antilles; the continent was just beyond. If you have got as far as the islands, it may be well, before you give up the search, to look at the sea-weeds and drift-wood, whether they do not come from the mainland. Having gathered and cooked the mussels, you might as well stay and eat them as to have another eat them and throw the shells after you. Charles Lamb discourseth about the mussel wisely: "Traveling is not good for us; we travel so seldom. How much more dignified leisure hath a mussel, glued to his impassable rocky limit, two inches square! He hears the tide roll over him backward and forward twice a day (as the Salisbury coach goes and returns in eight and forty hours), but knows better than to take an outside place on the top of it. He is the owl of the sea, Minerva's fish, the fish of wisdom." And yet the mussel can travel, and if detached will seek out a new location, and by means of its silken beard, or byssus threads, which it can weave in a few minutes, anchor itself anew to the rock. It has two enemies: The whelk, a sort of univalve mussel wolf, which bores a hole through the shell about the size of a pin, and sucks the life out; then there is a species of sea-gull which, when all other resources fail, plucks off the mussels, and, rising high enough, dashes them on the rocks; from which circumstance Æsop may, or may not, have invented his story of an eagle dashing a tortoise on the shining crown of a bald-headed man.

Yonder, where the surf frets the shore and pencils a dark line of kelp, look for the star-fish and the limpet, and for mosses in ultramarine and carmine such as no florist can match from his garden. And what is the sea but a treasure-house of palms and ferns, of corals, and of lilies which no eye hath seen, and royal highways, under whose arches there is an eternal procession of living things, and glorious mausoleums for the dead? This maritime discourse was somewhat abbreviated, because the youngster for whose benefit it had been made suddenly disappeared behind the rocks. He had begun some experiments on his own account. He had found out that the abalone which cleaves to the rocks has a wonderful suction, and the pinching of his finger between the shell and the rock, as in the vice of a blacksmith, extorted a wholesome yell and kept him in a grave and thoughtful frame of mind for five minutes. Anemones abound in all the rocky pools, spongy, unfolding at the top and closing quickly at the touch, the lowest form of sentient life, but knowing what is what. This youngster takes his second lesson in natural history by dropping in a mussel, when the anemone closes over it, and in a few minutes thereafter throws out an empty shell; but when the young rogue dropped in a stone, it was thrown out in a contemptuous way, as if the anemone had long ago understood the trick and was not to be deceived by naughty boys.

The star-fish comes in with the drift, as if he were altogether helpless; but, dull and inert as he seems, he watches tides and opportunities. Like the whelk, he loves the bivalve mollusk, but does not bore for it. There is a theory that he holds his five fingers affectionately around the clam or oyster, and then, by the aid of a sort of marine chloroform, secures an opening, when in goes one of the five fingers, and the mollusk is forced to shell out. There is a beautiful combination of persuasion and force. The sedative is tried first, and the pressure afterward. It is a pity that some such process could not be tried on that class of human mollusks whose shells have closed over their millions with an unrelenting grip. Some day their empty shells may be cast up on the other shore. It might be better for them that a star-fish should insert one of his fingers before the drift period begins.

In the chalk bluff, more than forty feet from high-water mark, is the vertebræ of a whale distinctly outlined. This monarch of the seas selected his tomb with some reference to the fitness of things. The Egyptian monarchs built for themselves granite tombs; but the whale lay down on the ooze, and the infusoria of five thousand years or more built around and above him. He was grandly inurned, and lifted up out of the sea by such a force as no living or dead Pharaoh could command. In the matter of royal sepulture, it is certain that the whale had an immense advantage. But after three or four thousand years, the defunct monarchs of sea and land are mainly valuable for bone-dust, and are rather poor fertilizers at best. From the hill one may see whales gambol in the Bay of Monterey, in the early Spring months. What a great laundry establishment these fellows might set up, if they only knew how to utilize their power! At present, these columns of spray blown into the horizon are only picturesque. There is a grave suspicion that the friend, whose Mongol servant blew the spray from his mouth into the sponge to be set for bread, would have much preferred that the whale had performed that office. Years ago, one of these monsters was seen floundering about in the bay all day long, as though in great distress. The following night he drifted ashore, dead. The great hulk had no mark of the sword-fish or the whaleman's lance. The sailors said that he was worried, teased, and finally hunted to death, by a fish called a "bummer." How strikingly human-like was the experience of the dead mammal!

There was a strange fascination about two wrecked vessels, whose timber heads could be seen above the sand. Sometimes, in a storm, they would get adrift. So weird like and mysteriously did they rise and fall on the surging sea, appearing and disappearing, thrusting their timbers out like arms imploring help, that one might fancy they were the spirits of these lost vessels coming back to protest against this broken rest. How strangely they accented the storm! When it subsided they would bring up at the old place, and the sand would bury them again. There was an odd genius in the town who claimed these wrecks by pre-emption. When his finances were low, and creditors pressed for small bills, he made his payments conditioned, as to time, on the coming of the next storm which would unbury the wrecks. Providence saved him a deal of hard shoveling, by raising the wind for him. Then he drew out copper bolts enough from the wreck to liquidate his bills, but gathered no surplus. Hath not many a mine been exhausted by indiscreet development? As long as that copper lasted, "Bob" paid his debts periodically. If he has not yet drawn his last copper bolt, he is still entitled to the financial confidence of this trading and huckstering world.

These round holes in the hard rocks are wrought deftly by the *Pholas*, a little bivalve, which, by means of its rasping shell and strong, elastic foot, keeps up the attrition, grinding away day and night until his excavation is perfect. It fits him on all sides, and he is content to live and die there. How much better is his condition than that of round men who have been trying all their lives to fit themselves into square holes, and square men who never could adjust themselves to round holes. The *Pholas* has found his place, and therefore may be ahead in the race. There was a famous theologian of the last century, who, sitting at his desk year after year, wrestling with problems which neither he nor any other mortal ever understood, ground the floor of his little study, by the attrition of his feet, until it was nearly worn through. His footprints are still preserved as sacred relics. Nor ought the inquiry to be pressed now whether the hole which the *Pholas* wrought with his foot, or the hole which the theologian ground with his foot, was the better or more permanent one. If the question is at all pertinent, it may be ripe for an answer a thousand years hence.

When the tide is out, one may find the razor-fish, so called because the shell resembles the handle of a razor. If laid hold of suddenly, the chances are that before he can be drawn out he will slip out of his shell, leaving that empty in the hand, while the "soul and essence" of him has gone down half a fathom into the sand. Yet he is not more slippery than many an individual, who, when pressed to do some magnanimous deed in behalf of the community, slips out of his shell, and, losing the grip, you can no more find the soul and essence of him than you can find the soul of this razor-fish, which has gone deep into the muck and sand. In either instance, the empty shell is only the sign of the thing wanted.

If it were not for this eternal scene-shifting, the monotony of the sea might be oppressive. But every change of the wind, and every drifting cloud across the sky, gives a new blending of color and tone. If to-morrow the south wind shall blow, or a gale come piping down from the north, the face of the deep will have been created anew, as much so, in an æsthetic view, as if it had been poured out for the first time on the surface of the globe. Is there not a perpetual series of creations on both sea and land? The waters are taken up in the clouds, and poured out again. Mountains are disintegrated, and go down to the valleys, but other mountains are lifted up out of the sea and out of the arid plains. Climbing a hill, more than four hundred feet above the surface of the water, and five miles inland from the present shore line, one may find thousands of marine shells, many of mollusks not yet extinct as species, and read on the face of this conglomerate, as in open volume, the record of a physical creation, whether by the subsidence of the sea or the elevation of the land, as fresh, geologically, as if all this had occurred but a century ago. This world of waters creates no sense of isolation. Observe, too, that whoever has been born and bred by the shore will evermore look out on the sea and be glad. A sail is better than a horse, and the breaking of the waves hath more majesty and a diviner music than any organ touched by human hands. *Mem.*: the man who has gone over the rocks, and is filling his pockets with mussels in a furtive sort of a way, is from the interior. He wants salting. He is looking out drift wood, and will strike a match presently. Let him fancy, if he will, that his feast is fit for the gods. To-night he will probably dream that one of these wrecks, covered with barnacles and sea-weed, has rolled over, and is lying athwart his capacious diaphragm.

The Patriarch went out into the fields at eventide. Was it any the worse for him that his meditations were gilded with a touch of romance? What if he thought less of the lilies of the field, and more of the veiled lily from Nahor? Was not that human? So we go down to the seashore as the soft twilight comes on apace, and think it no worse that the voices of lovers blend with the cadence of waters. If there is no higher inspiration for them, let Isaac speak to Rebecca. It is little to them that there is a blush in the horizon, and that a moment ago the sea was opalescent, and the mountains put on and off their royal vestments of purple.

This homestead by the sea was an accident. It was the result of a bit of face-tiousness, that had a solemn termination, as it were. Riding past the court-house in Santa Cruz, nineteen years ago, when that town had not as many hundred people, the wag of a sheriff was dividing his time between crying a ranch at public sale, to close an estate, and whittling a stick. No bids for the last hour. Would the citizen on horseback halt a minute and accommodate him with a bid, just to relieve the dullness of the occasion? The last bid was raised five dollars. What did that madcap of a sheriff do but slap his hands together and declare that the estate was sold. There have been earthquakes which were inconveniently sudden, and thunder-claps from a clear sky; but such an investiture of real property had not been known in many a day. The sheriff shut up his jack-knife; the bystanders closed theirs, and they all went round the corner, as they said, to consult a barometer—a proceeding which that official never did fully explain. When one has been over-taken by a surprise, a climax, or even a joke, which has at the bottom of it such a flavor of real estate, it is best to sleep on it for one night, and take a fresh view of the situation on the following day. Does not the ideal country estate in some way enter into the sleeping or waking dreams of most sanguine men? There are to be many broad acres, parks, and fountains, orchards drooping with fruit; vineyards creeping up the hillsides; a trout stream in which "chubs" greatly abound; a capacious mansion, with hospitable doors swinging open as if by instinct on the approach of friends; barns filled with fragrant hay; thoroughbred stock, from the horse down to the dog and cat; Alderney cows, coming up at night with cream in their horns, mild-eyed and gentle, with breath as sweet as the wild clover they had eaten; gilt-edged butter, not handed round in pats as large as a shilling, for admiration, but set forth in solid cubes, like gold which had been honestly assayed and run into ingots; strawberries perennial, and always smothered in cream; bell-flowers and pippins, ripening in the Autumn sun; scientific farming, not for profit, but just to demonstrate how it can be done; long, tranquil days, restful and full of indescribable peace, when bees go droning by, and the perfume of the orchard comes in at the open windows. That is pretty nearly an outline of your dream, with some minor variation of details thrown in; such, for instance, as a great chamber looking toward the rising sun, where the one epic poem of the nineteenth century is to be written. Are there some twinges of pain about the heart that this dream has never been quite realized? Consider for a moment that heaven, so far as it relates to this world, is for the most part an ideal conception. It is not what one has reduced to possession, but what he hopes to have. Now, one can put a great deal of heaven into the ideal country home, and not realize largely on the investment. If the strawberries cost a dollar apiece, and the favorite horse has a trick of putting his heels up toward the stars, the chickens stagger about with the gapes, and the phylloxera browns the vineyard as if a subterranean fire had been burning at the roots, these touches of realism may chasten the expectations somewhat, and at the same time serve to plant the amateur farmer more firmly on his feet. It is a pity that the world could not be enriched by the experience of the gilt-edged farmer from the city. What is most wanted is a book of failures—an honest filling in of the blanks between the ideal and real country life.

A survey of the new purchase disclosed a number of particulars; and, among others, that a dead man's pre-emption claim, when sold under the form of law, passes a rather shadowy title to the buyer. It was needful to become a constructive pre-emptor, and to exhort a number of impenitent squatters to early penitence and reformation. The Saxon's hunger for land is generally matched by his appetite for land stealing. If two parcels of land of equal area and value be shown him, one already claimed and the other open to settlement, the chances are that this descendant of ancient land-robbers would much prefer to pounce on the land already occupied, and fight it out. If he is not reconstructed in his inmost soul, he will always be wanting his neighbor's vineyard. The new purchase met all æsthetic requirements. It was on the edge of the town, and hardly more than a mile from the sea. It had a grove in the foreground, a trout stream on either side, with a fringe of tall redwoods, a backing of mountains, and a water view comprising the whole of Monterey Bay, and as much of the ocean as the eye could reduce to constructive possession. Not a fence to mark a boundary; but the two-room shanty, with its great stone chimney on the outside, loomed up like a palace. There was a fire-place which yawned like an immense cave. An old rifle-barrel, planted in the chimney, served well enough as a crane. The opening at the top was liberally adjusted for astronomical observations, but had been slightly abridged by the nest of a pair of gray wood squirrels, which kept up a perpetual racing on the dry roof at night.

It is not probable that the primitive man had any such house to await his coming; and having his constitution adjusted to a tropical climate at the outset, he had little use for a stone fire-place where the back-log lasted a week. It would furnish a curious commentary on the evolution of dwellings if one could establish the fact that the first house was built of *adobes*, like those which one now sees along the bluff of the Branciforte, and which have more than one quality of the perfect country house. A breastwork of earth might have been raised first, to break off tempests; afterward, it would have four sides, then perhaps a thatch of palm leaves—and the primitive *adobe* dwelling stood in its glory. In such a habitation the sun could not smite by day, and only the fleas could smite powerfully at night. If any learned archæologist finds fault with this theory, let him make a better one out of *adobes* if he can.

It was an odd circumstance that the grove had been the chosen place for many a camp meeting, the board buildings still remaining; while on the opposite side an eccentric African had occupied for many years a hut, and led a sort of mystic life. He was skillful in compounding simples, the potency of which was greatly increased by his incantations. It was even said that he had the gift of hoo-dooing, and always kept the roughs at bay by threatening to fix his eye on them. There was a trace of orthodoxy in his methods—since, if the wicked cannot be won by love, they can sometimes be scared into decency by sending the devil after them. Here were signs of grace on one side, and diabolism on the other. But neither effected much in "Squabble Hollow," two miles beyond. It is a pity that the African had not done a little hoo-dooing up there among the pioneers, so that the reign of peace might have set in at an earlier day. It is quiet enough now, because Time, with his scythe, has cut a clean swath there.

If one has planted his own orchard, he will eat the fruit with greater satisfaction. He will have an affection for the trees which he once carried under his arm, and will trim them tenderly in the spring. Whoever ate the cherries which he bought in the market with such secret satisfaction as those which he plucked from his own trees in the early morning? If your neighbor invites you to his cherry orchard, he honors you above kings. It is doubtful if royalty ever poised itself on a rickety chair, or reached for cherries so deftly as that school girl, who read her graduating essay, with pendent blue ribbons, last month. She is not greatly changed now, except that her mouth has increased about a hundred per cent. Every tree which one sets with his own hands is better than those which the hireling and stranger have set. He establishes secret relations with it, communes with it, eats of the fruit as if the tree itself rejoiced in bestowing such a benediction. When the apples fall to the ground, in the still autumn day, it is as if they dropped from the opening heavens. Every one is the symbol of wisdom, and hath, in its malic acid, a subtile essence, which carries health to the morbid liver. And no individual is ever wise when that organ is in trouble, or, at least, he has an unhappy way of expressing his wisdom. From this sanitary point of view, it will accord with a healthy conscience if a little cider mill is set up under the wide-branching oak hard by. If you have any scruples, you need not taste of the cider, but you can smell of the pomace, and note how the bees and yellow-jackets are drawn to it for honey.

The bees go in a straight line to a knot-hole in the dead top of a redwood tree. The taking up of a wild swarm, which had stored honey in another tree, was not a happy experiment. When the tree came down, there was a black, boiling mass of enraged bees. No lack of honey. But if one wishes to know what is meant by the "iron entering into the soul," let a dozen bees go under his necktie, and prod him along his back—the last one, by way of a tiger, prodding the tip of his nose, because at that very instant one must sneeze or die. How can one tell what is sweet except there be some bitterness in contrast? It was evident that old dog "Samson," who dropped his tail and yelled when the bees lit on him, was not given to much philosophical reflection; but the speed of that disconsolate cur was mightily helped on his way back to the kennel. If an invitation were now extended to him to take up another hive, he would do nothing more than wave his tail and send regrets.

That platform in the grove is maintained for the benefit of free speech, with reasonable limitations. Clerical and political orators have had their day there. In short, it is the platform of all nations, newly consecrated every summer by the rhythmic feet and gleesome voices of childhood. Then, if ever, the oak and madrono spread their branches of perpetual green over such more tenderly, as symbols of the immortal freshness of youth. Is not this succession of life from chaos eternal, and the race itself only in its infancy? Neither the woodman's axe nor the fire could take the vitality out of that redwood stump, for the saplings have sprung out of its clefts, and the old roots are sending these new spires up toward the heavens. As little does the destruction of a nation affect the genesis of the race, or its everlasting succession. The orchard is the symbol of peace, abundance, the mellowness of life. It is the sign of a gentle civilization grafted on to the wildness of nature. The wild blackberry and strawberry, which grow along the fences and hedgerows, have an aboriginal flavor. When they are domesticated they are a hundredfold better. The wild trees of the forest take to themselves new qualities when set in the open grounds. The ship built of "pasture oak" is a better craft, because the toughness of fiber of such trees was gained in the open field, where they had given shelter to ruminating cows. Was not the yew tree, which grew about the ancestral homes generations ago, chosen for the cross-bow because of its toughness and elasticity? This solitary ash by the fence is more lithe and graceful for its introduction to domestic life; and this wide-branching oak before the door, casting now its shadows aslant, made handsome obeisance to the earthquake, sweeping the ground with its lateral branches. Not a fracture of one of its elastic limbs; but that ancient stone chimney rumbled fearfully, and stood apart in moody isolation. When the dog abandons the civilized community and hears no human speech, he loses his bark. The lowest type of humanity has only a few guttural sounds. The civilized master follows the condition of his dog—that is, if he be cast on some solitary island, he gradually loses his speech. Dog and man have finally gone back to dumb nature. Why is the fruit of the ancient pear tree, standing by some deserted homestead of ante-revolutionary days, more acrid and pungent than it was a hundred years ago? It had lost association with human kind. If one could grasp the sweeter subtleties of Nature, he might find a gracious accord, a point of sympathetic contact, where the mellowness of the individual, the rich and generous juices of his nature, give a finer quality to the fruits of the trees which he has planted. Something may come back to him, also, in the aroma of the orchard, helping him by its fragrance to a gentler and more thoughtful life.

SUBURBAN ETCHINGS.

IT accords with the folk-lore, or traditions of the "Hill," that one must not offer violence to a black cat. Now it happened that in the season of spring chickens—in the very callow time of their existence—a vagrant cat installed himself in the garden. Charcoal was grey in contrast with the depth of his blackness; and his yellow eyes were flanked by jowls indicating that he fared sumptuously. If a cat of this hue is a symbol of evil, why not induce him to move on at once? "Bridget" was questioned for a satisfactory answer. "Because you mustn't. It is bad luck to harm a black cat." And so this superstition from the heart of the African continent was respected for a time. There might be some occult influence by which the cat propagated the superstition; creating it and living, as it were, in its very atmosphere. Hoodooing possibly is not confined to Africans. It has some relation to blackness, midnight, weird and mysterious eyes. This prowling feline may have in him the spirit of mischief. A symbol of evil may sometimes be the thing itself. It is a strange custom to mourn for lost friends by wearing black. What more natural interpretation than that the wearer also is dead? Whereas the "heathen" have hit upon a better symbol, wearing white for the loss of friends, signifying that they have entered into light, that the world itself is all luminous for the living.

Now that cat, the spirit and essence of darkness, the forerunner of diabolism, was true to the symbol. What did he do but leap over a high fence every morning and take from the inclosure the tenderest of spring chickens. Then an hour afterward he would go down the garden walk for a greeting, as if he were not a knave and a hypocrite, arching his back and curving his tail beautifully, rubbing his sleek coat against one and looking up in the face as much as to say, "The only honest trades in the world are yours and mine." It is true that the business economy of the world is mainly a system of reprisals. But there ought to be a spiritual economy which should teach something better. It is evident that this cat must be converted with other than spiritual weapons. In a millennial sense shotguns, no doubt, may become "organ pipes of peace," and even now they may be used to project a sermon to a considerable distance. One by one that brood of chickens disappeared, and another was just coming off. A neighbor was consulted as to the best manner of getting around the superstition that no harm must be done to a black cat. The case was plain enough. He had a beautiful breech-loading shotgun, costing, he suggested, a hundred and twenty dollars. All that was necessary to be done in the premises was to exhort that marauder with that gun. He would show us how to use it. Then followed a drill in its use. The cartridges went in at the breech, an eye was to be squinted along the barrel—and then came the crisis. What a beautiful implement! And how wonderful the contrast with the old Queen's arm, the relic of revolutionary days stored in the garret, with its flint lock, priming wire and muzzle, into which went five fingers of powder and shot, and one of wads! That gun, the use of which was always interdicted to small boys, had been let down from the garret window many a time by a toe-string manufactured for the occasion, and the first hint which maternal government got of that sleight of hand was a report in the nearest woods, which all the heavens echoed to the old homestead. That honest revolutionary piece would not lie. It spoke the truth even if we had to suffer the consequences. The draft made on a clump of hazel bushes near by, was the serious part of the business. But it abides in the memory that no red squirrel running on a ziz-zag fence was wholly safe when that Queen's arm was pointed at him.

The breech-loader was taken down and stored in the library for an aggravated occasion. It came in a few days. The man of all work came bowling up the walk red and wrathful. "That old son of perdition has got another chicken!" Now then, his time had come. He shall be swept with the besom of destruction. Superstitions go this day for nothing. A hundred and twenty dollar shotgun, silver mounted, and a patent cartridge! "Rest it across my back, 'Squire, and take good aim. Aim for his shoulder, and don't kill the chicken in his mouth." —"Did you fetch the cat?" Well, not exactly. The old superstition that day had a powerful effect. That cat dropped the chicken, though, and ran toward the gunner as if to salute him, and then leaped over a ten-feet fence and disappeared. That was not all. There were four chickens feeding in the grass beyond, every one of which was laid out cold, and a fifth was struck in the head and had the blind staggers so that it was counted in with the dead. There had been a little variance in the "besom of destruction" which operated in favor of that mysterious cat. Then there was the salutation of Bridget: "Didn't I tell you that it is bad luck to kill a black cat!" "Well, I haven't killed him by a long way. But you might go down in the back lot and gather up an apron full of spring chickens." That gun was returned with thanks. It was an elegant piece. But, somehow, it didn't work like the Queen's arm. The next day that cat returned as if nothing had happened, and took the regular toll of a chicken a day. For a whole year more these depredations went on at intervals, regulated by the supply of young chickens. Here was enterprise. A hundred-dollar chicken yard, constructed and arranged on "scientific principles," was just adequate for the supply of one black cat, on which no impression could be made with a breech-loader, while chickens were bought every week in the market to meet the home demand! In this extremity a new plan was evolved.

A cash premium—a new dollar from the mint—shall go for the destruction of this particular cat and all successors. Robert, the utility man, soon claimed the dollar. He had exhorted the sleek old hypocrite with a hoe-handle, and brought him to sudden repentance.

"It is bad luck to kill a black cat," said Bridget the next morning; "and you didn't kill him, neither." Well, I paid Robert a premium of a dollar, and he took him off. "Hang all superstitions."

"But the black cat is down in the garden now."

There was that thieving rascal, or a duplicate, at the old business. Robert offered to show the original underground. The premium business was continued, and went into the monthly statement. No sooner was one taken off than another appeared, provided always that it was not the original vagabond. The same predatory habits, the same midnight and diabolical expression, the same decimation in the chicken yard. What did it all mean? There was some occult diabolism that could not be explained. "Didn't I tell you," says Bridget, with an air of triumph, "that you can't kill a black cat."

No, I can't, with a breech-loader. But Robert is drawing a regular premium. The black cat premium fund was exhausted. Now, state your account, my boy. "Well, I have killed *five*, upon honor, and have my eye upon another one." There was a suspicion that the original was still there. But the superstition vanished in the clear light of day when it was shown that number six had a little fleck of white between the four legs. But the depredations still go on, and you cannot convince the honest old house-servant that a black cat has ever been killed—and looking out into the garden just now, as that sleek black rascal lies in the grass, with a waving motion of his tail and his yellow eye fixed upon a callow brood, it is clearer than ever before that the succession of black cats is eternal. They do not come in single file, but sun themselves on the fences by the half dozen, run over the greenhouse, breaking panes of glass, climb up on the outside to the gable window of the barn, flit across the garden walks at twilight, conceal themselves under the low shrubbery, as if defying all efforts at dislodgement. Then there is the comment of Patrick, our neighbor's utility man: "They know the char-*acter* you've made with that gun."

Nor was it a mitigating circumstance that a sympathizing friend proposed to regulate the succession of cats by sending over a small half-grown terrier. If well brought up, he would keep the peace in the interest of spring chickens. He did occasionally run the black vagrants to the trees handsomely. But as an incidental diversion, he would lay out half a dozen chickens on any fine morning. Where was the gain? Cats could be exhorted with a shotgun, at least there was one experiment of that kind. But when "Towser" was exhorted with a switch, a wail went up from the Hill. It was as if the spirits of all the dogs in Christendom had united to pierce the heavens. So great a noise for so small a catastrophe! But this elementary education cannot be interrupted on account of noises. There is a Hindoo proverb that you cannot get the crook out of a dog's tail by mollifying appliances. But what was needed in that particular case was to get the crook out of his intellect. It ought to have been settled long ago, as a principal of moral and mental philosophy, that you cannot beat honesty and virtue into men or dogs. And so this young canine rascal will come back to do to-morrow what he has done to-day. Does the boy rob bird's nests or plum trees any the less because he gets a sprouting now and then? He has in his moral system a thousand years of inherited aptitude for such predatory excursions.

The moulting season having come, the "chicken lot" looks as if several feather beds had been emptied there. There is less crowing and apparently more time given to meditation and introspection. The old rooster and his harem are now in undress, and a hint has been given that domestic eggs will be scarce for the next month. A young chick that learned to crow hardly more than a month ago, and eats from the hand with fine audacity, has just begun to balance his accounts. He is in full dress—his first suit, as it were—and is not subject to the moulting process at present. But having been under the tyranny of the patriarch who has now lost his tail, the younger one calls him to account daily. There is a hint of retributive justice here. All tyrants ought to have some part of their accounts settled in this world. By way of example, it might be better if the settlements were very complete. After all, there are very few tyrants who manage to get out of the world without a partial accounting with humanity. Now and then, it is measure for measure, the tyrant having his heaped up a little by way of emphasis. That last reflection is made clearer by the way that young rooster, in his juvenile dress, persists in settling his grievances. He knows nothing of the quality of magnanimity, which suggests that when an adversary has had a sound drubbing he should be let off with a mild regret that any such chastening had been necessary. There is little probability that the quality of mercy will be strained at present. Although, when a tramp called at the kitchen door, unkempt, belated and besotted, the compassionate Bridget set him out a generous breakfast. But when he complained that the coffee was not hot, the quality of mercy was strained which withheld the firing of the poker and coal scuttle at his head. The asceticism of the modern tramp, and the delicacy and exacting nature of his tastes, constitute the latest problem in sociology. It is strange, too, that his moulting season should last the year round. His laying off season never ends. His gains are in inverse proportion to his industry. It might be well to inquire whether there is not a secret profit in cultivating incapacity for work. This Christian Bedouin gets all he needs without effort. But daily I see a man who has acquired ten millions, and wants more. I know not which is the better off. The one appears to be going forward to an eternity of wants. Suppose this capacity for wanting things to increase in geometrical ratio—it may be necessary to mortgage the universe for his convenience. The other is going back on the track, lightening the dead weight as he goes, shedding his superfluous clothes by the wayside, getting down to the level of a ruminating animal, rejoicing in the fragrance of hay stacks at night and the freedom of hospitable kitchens by day. If there is nothing better than to delve for clothes and wooden palaces, it were as well that there should be more moulting. Who knows but the tramp reposing in the sun, his blood enriched thereby, his person made a little more fragrant by the redolence of the hay stack, may not gain a fresh stock of vitality quite needful for this languishing world? The profoundest philosopher of modern times surprised the world with a treatise devoted mainly to clothes. It is not given to know the day on which the profounder philosopher will come and surprise the world by showing the absurdity of clothes worn in conformity to any conventional requirements. Society is forever moulting, putting off and on, and is not happy. But the Patagonian covers his epidermis with mud to protect him from cold, and is happy, at least there is no evidence to the contrary. After all, there was a savor of health in the cynicism which inspired the sturdy old Greek to live in his tub when at home, and to hunt for an honest man with a lantern in the open day. It is nowhere stated that he found him.

There is an ancient Spanish custom of planting the seed of fruit which has been eaten. It is a way of pronouncing a benediction for the good received—not in empty words, but by a thoughtful and beneficent act. One has eaten of the fruit that another has planted, and he is glad; he will also plant that another may eat. Were that custom perpetuated the world over, evermore there would be fruit by the wayside. The highways and byways would not be cursed with barrenness and dust, but fringed with the mulberry and apple, with silent salutations for every weary traveler who would put forth his hand and eat. What matters it that the tree planted to-day shall never overarch and protect you from the smiting sun?—shall never drop its golden fruit by your side? Shall we not read by the light of eternal day that every tree thus planted has brought its benediction to the world? Is it little that others had planted for us, that we should forget to plant again? The patriarch entertained an angel unaware. How many angels might be entertained by one goodly orchard? Or, at least, such as by grace of speech, of mind, and manner, have already received the divine stamp. The heavens have no message for the destroyer; but they have one of peace for those who plant and build wisely on the earth.

It is a notable fact that all the deciduous trees, as well as all the rose bushes which are within the range of suburban observation, have a dormant season about mid-summer. Neither the sun, the south wind, nor water at the roots, can wholly prevent this intervening period of rest. In their own time and way they awake, as it were, to newness of life. In this dormant season they are storing energy for a new development. It is drawn from the sun, the atmosphere, and the nursing earth. When they have accumulated fresh stores there is a new wealth of blossom and foliage. Something analogous to this divine order reaches over from matter to mind. There are dormant seasons—periods of infertility—when the chemistry of heaven and earth is needed to overcome this barrenness. The artist dreams and touches not the fresh canvas on his easel. The poet wanders aimlessly in wider pastures, content to see the bees come and go, and the lupins and wild poppies nod to each other on the hillside. It is the ruminant season, when it is needful that one should digest what has been stored up within. Doth not the land lying in summer fallow gain new fertility? The unclothed land going so near to barrenness shall surely be clothed upon in the coming spring-time. It is well now if one may lie down and dream that the heavens were studded for him alone; and that the west wind of autumn, bearing the perfume of a hundred orchards, comes to him from a land of eternal fruitage. Even now the young leaves are starting on the rose bushes; the period of second growth has already begun. The pear begins to blush under the rays of a September sun; and a strange lily among the ineffable white of the callas, has gone all aflame, as if sainthood and bleeding martyrdom were never far apart.

LITERATURE AND ART.[2]

IF one may find by the way-side in early springtime so much as a harebell or dandelion, a springing blade of grass or an unfolding bud, as much real satisfaction may be drawn from these scant treasures as from the more abounding fullness of summer, or the mellow ripeness of autumn. In all that relates to education, literature and art, it is early springtime here. What would you have more than some wayside evidences of the serene summer yet to follow, and an intellectual fruitage, of which the gold and purple of the vintage are but the faintest symbols? What is a quarter of a century in the life of a commonwealth, to the rounded centuries which have matured the great universities of Europe, or even the two centuries which have enriched Harvard and Yale? The canvas tents of '49, pitched on the sandy slopes of the peninsula, promised no great city, no perfected system of common schools, no academies and seminaries, and no university planted at Berkeley, in sight from a city of more than a quarter of a million inhabitants. The dissolving gravel beds of a placer mine and the arid plains, were neither symbols of permanence nor of bread. What could you expect in this stress of humanity, even though the agglomerated community were not lacking in some of the best and bravest of all lands?

There can be no beginning of a commonwealth until a Divine Providence begins to set the solitary in families. Homes, children, the economies of domestic life, the commonwealth of husband and wife, the law of the household, and that human providence which grows tender and thoughtful with each young and dependent life—these are precedent conditions of the future state.

It was most fitting that a graduate of one of the oldest colleges in the country should have opened the first public school in California. Thomas Douglas, a graduate of Yale College, began a public school in San Francisco on the 3d day of April, 1848. It was a good beginning. But when a few months later nearly the whole population had, drifted away to the mines, Douglas was left high and dry on the sand hills.

All true scholarship has breadth and catholicity. Let not ours be impeached by ignoring what others have done in the domain of letters and science. The fact is none the less significant, that the public school, with its canvas roof, and three scholars, in 1849, is crowned by the University of California to-day.

Possibly, the pioneer educators builded better than they knew. Douglas, the master of arts of Yale, setting the first stakes in the sand hills—Marvin, the first State Superintendent of Public Schools, who, having made a campaign against

---

[2] Delivered on "Assembly Day," at the University of California.

the Indians, turned over his emoluments to the school fund—Brayton, who conducted for years the most successful preparatory school in the State, a brave, patient and lovable man, whose life went out all too soon in the midst of his noble work—Durant, who, beginning at the foundations, saw the University with the clear vision of a prophet, and lived to see the fruition of his hopes—the gentle and profound scholar, the dignified president, the wise and firm civil magistrate, who, in the richness of his intellect, the purity of his soul, and the steadfastness of his friendship, was more than president, magistrate, or scholar. Tompkins, as a legislator and as regent, worked with unflagging zeal for the University, and fitly crowned that work by endowing, out of his moderate fortune, the first professorship. When he had made his last public speech in behalf of the institution for which he had wrought so well, it remained for him to enter into the sacred guild of those pioneers who had gone a little before. Gilman, the second president, whose organizing mind grasped every detail of the University, who wrought effectively for it by day, and planned wisely for it by night—a man of rare executive ability, who seemed half unconscious of his own power to influence men in behalf of the great interests for which he wrought. Let it be said of him that he bore himself in his high office with a patience and dignity befitting the Christian gentleman and accomplished scholar. Such a man rarely misses his place, because he is a citizen of the world of letters. It is here for a few years, and on the other side of the country for more. But here or there, I think he will never need a better testimonial than that which his work will offer.

Some good work has also been done in a scientific way. The geological survey of this State was arrested by the impatience of the people for immediate results. The topographical survey alone, than which nothing better has ever been done in this country, was more than an equivalent for the entire outlay. There will come a time when the practical value of such an enterprise will be better understood. The physical problems in a single State like California could not be solved in half a century. Was it well to ask a scientific commission to solve them, and publish the results in a few months?

The public journal, as a factor in education, is here, as elsewhere, the outgrowth of our civilization. It embodies the passions, caprices and enterprises of the community. In its best estate it gives the history of the world for one day. In its poorest estate it is content with a patent outside, the puffing of some mountebank, and the abuse of rivals. But at the close of this quarter century, the only complete history of the rise and progress of this commonwealth is that which the newspapers contain. I have seen an artist sketch an accurate likeness of his friend on his thumb-nail. But the modern newspaper every day sketches the likeness, the pulse, and the throbbing heart of the civilized world.

Just as the ideal state is something far in advance of the actual, so the ideal newspaper is something far better than exists on this side of the continent. Here, as elsewhere, it is largely the product of steamships, railroads and telegraphs. But the journal of the future will, after all, be very much what the community makes it. It is the child of civilization, going forward with the community to a better condition, or going backward with it to coarseness and barbarism. The best newspaper a hundred years ago was a poor affair. A hundred years hence, the journal of to-day will probably be viewed with as much interest for what it lacks, as for what it contains.

Our ideal newspaper will pander to no mean prejudices. It will be no generator of slang phrases. It will not murder honest English. It will have ripe and well-digested opinions. It will not truckle to base men. It will not sneer at religion. It will keep its editorial columns above all just suspicion of purchase. It will leave garbage in the gutter. It will assail no man unjustly, nor fear to defend any man or interest because he or it may be obscure or unpopular. No good citizen will fear the honest journal of the future, and no bad man will like it.

Observe how the outer bark of the madrono and eucalyptus, with the coming of every Summer, bursts, rolls up, and falls to the ground as so much rubbish. That is a sign of expanding life. A great deal of newspaper rubbish to-day is a sign of growth. The outer rind and husk of things fall to the ground by that vital force which is continually developing a larger and nobler life in the community. No man will hereafter go to the head of this profession without fair scholarship, a wide range of observation, a large capacity, to deal in a general way with human affairs, and that keen insight which catches the spirit and essence of this on-going life. Most difficult of all is a certain power of statement which no school can teach, and without which the highest plane of the journalist cannot be reached. Your long story will not be heard. The world is waiting for the man of condensation. Tell it in few words. If one can master this high eclecticism of thought and statement, I know of no more promising field for young men to-day than journalism. If one cannot, the potato field, in a season of blight, is quite as promising.

Without this broader culture for the journalist, there will be great danger that the exigencies of his work will make him a superficial man. The habit will grow upon him of touching merely the surface of things. He will come to think that, as his journal is only for the day, his errors are for the day also. The habit of careful investigation and exactness of thought and statement, will be discarded for random guesses and the temporary expedients of the hour. Nothing but the balancing influence of generous culture will arrest this lapsing tendency. It will be disclosed in platitudes and commonplaces; in writing against space, and in that dreadful amplitude which buries a thought under a mountain of verbiage.

One cannot fail to note that the newspaper has been gradually encroaching on the domain of literature. It has absorbed monthly magazines or forced publishers to resort to illustrations—to a sort of picture-book literature for grown-up children. It has driven the lumbering quarterlies into smaller fields and diminished their relative importance. The average citizen craves the news from a journal having the very dew of the morning and of the evening upon it. It must come to him damp and limp, bringing whatever is best at the smallest possible cost. The newspaper is the herald of the new era. Its errand must be swift, its statements compact, and its thought eclectic and comprehensive.

Three thousand years ago, one of the grand old prophets spoke mysteriously of the "living spirit in the wheels." Was it other than the modern newspaper thrown off by the pulsing of the great cylinder press? But observe that through yonder Golden Gate, which the sun and the stars and the lamps of men glorify day and night, the devil-fish comes sailing up, and is no whit concerned whether his accursed *tentacula* close around saint or sinner. Is it not the fittest symbol of a public journal conducted by ignorant and unscrupulous men? Rather would you not choose, as a more fitting symbol of the ideal journal, one of the small globules of quicksilver which you shall find on any of these encircling hills, so powerless to draw to it an atom of filth or rubbish, but ever attracting the smallest particle of incorruptible silver and gold?

It can hardly have escaped notice that California, during this quarter-century, has produced more humorists, and more of that literature which is essentially humorous, than all the rest of the country. It may be difficult to trace to any outward sources the inspiration of so much wit. Does it lie in the odd contrasts and strange situations which so often confront the observer here? Nor has this facetiousness depended at all for its development upon any degree of prosperity. In fact, the boldest and bravest challenge which has ever been given to adverse fortune here, has been by the gentle humorists who have suffered from her slings and arrows. It is said: "Cervantes smiled Spain's chivalry away." But these modern satirists made faces at bad fortune; they lampooned her and defied her to do her utmost. The more miserable they ought to have been, the happier they were. They found a grotesque and comic side to the most sober facts. They were facetious when there was small stock in the larder and smaller credit at the banker's. They smiled at the very grimness of evil fortune until she fled, and, in doing this, they half-unconsciously tickled the midriff of the world. A ripple of laughter ran over the surface of society. It sometimes made slow progress when it here and there met a mountain of obtuseness. But wit is wit; and what difference does it make if, failing to see the point, some people laugh next year instead of this? I will not be distressed because my friend does not, to this day, see how the immortal "Squibob" conquered his adversary at San Diego by falling underneath him and inserting his nose between his teeth. Nor does it greatly concern me that he does not assent to the proposition that John Phœnix, having made a national reputation by editing the San Diego *Herald* for one week, was the greatest journalist of modern times. If reputation is the measure of greatness, Phœnix is to this day without a peer. He made the very desert sparkle with his wit. He was a humorous comet, shooting across the dull horizon of pioneer life. Men looked up and wondered whence it came and whither it had gone.

Possibly, there is something favorable to the play of humor in a greater freedom from conventional limitations. If one grows into this larger liberty, or is translated into it, a flavor of freshness comes to pervade all the intellectual life. A certain spontaneity of expression, a spring, a rioting song of gladness, are some of the signs of this more abounding life. In homely phrase, we say there is a flavor of the soil about it. It might, therefore, have been necessary that Mark Twain should sleep on this soil, and should have a wide range of pioneer experiences, before he could become the prince of grotesque humorists. He got up suddenly from the very soil which in its secret laboratory colors the olive and the orange, and began to make the world laugh. With a keen sense of the symmetry and harmony of things, he had a keener perception of all the shams and ridiculous aspects of life. His pungent gospel of humor is as sanitary as a gentle trade-wind. He knew a better secret than the old alchemists. Every time he made the world laugh he put a thousand ducats into his pocket. But never until he had slept in his blankets, had been robbed on the "Divide," and had learned the delicate cookery of a miner's cabin, could he do these things. But now he cannot even weep at the tomb of his ancestor, Adam, without moving the risibles of half the world. He has also a finer touch and flavor, not of the rankest soil, but of that which gives the aroma and delicate bouquet to the rarest mountain-side vintage. When this man had tried his wit on a Californian audience and had won an approving nod, he had an endorsement that was good in any part of the English-speaking world.

Of a more subtile wit and a finer grain was Harte, who did his best work as a humorist in California. All his earlier triumphs were won here. His subsequent indorsement in a wider field was only an affirmation of this earlier public judgment.

Sometimes in the thicket one may come upon a wild mocking bird which is running up the gamut of its riotous burlesque upon the song of every other bird, and the sound of every living thing in the forest. But when all this is done, that mocking bird will sometimes give out a song which none other can match with its melody. As much as this, and more, lay within the range of this poet-satirist. His mocking had, however, a deep and salient meaning in it. When Truthful James rises to explain in what respect Ah Sin is peculiar, he has a higher purpose than merely to show the overreaching cunning of this bronzed heathen,

"With a smile that was child-like and bland."

So long as Ah Sin and his race could be plucked and despoiled at will, he provoked no antagonisms. But when he overmatched the sharpness of his spoilers, we have this tale, with its moral:

"Then I looked up at Nye;
And he gazed upon me;
And he rose with a sigh,
And said, 'Can this be?
We are ruined by Chinese cheap labor!'
And he went for that heathen Chinee."

Every demagogue in the State, who had rung the changes on the evils of cheap labor, felt the thrust; and it is doubtful if one of them has forgiven Harte to this day.

The dogmatism and intolerant assumption which sometimes become rampant in scientific societies, is thus punctured by Truthful James, in his description of "The Society upon the Stanislaus:"

"But first I would remark that it is not a proper plan
For any scientific gent to whale his fellow-man,
And if a member don't agree with his peculiar whim,
To lay for that same member for to 'put a head' on him."

When Jones undertook to prove that certain fossil bones were from one of his lost mules, then the trouble began:

> "Now I hold it is not decent for any scientific gent
> To say another is an ass—at least to all intent;
> Nor should the individual who happens to be meant,
> Reply by heaving rocks at him, to any great extent.
>
> "Then Abner Dean of Angel's raised a point of order, when
> A chunck of old red sandstone took him in the abdomen,
> And he smiled a sickly smile, and curled up on the floor,
> And the subsequent proceedings interested him no more.
>
> "For in less time than I write it every member did engage
> In a warfare with the remnants of the paleozoic age;
> And the way they heaved those fossils in their anger was a sin,
> Till the skull of an old mammoth caved the head of Thompson in."

When the supposed pliocene skull, found in Calaveras County, had developed a good deal of scientific quackery, Harte, in his "Geological Address," makes the skull declare that it belonged to Joe Bowers, of Missouri, who had fallen down a shaft. For six months thereafter no theorist was able to discuss the character of that fossil with a sober countenance. No Damascus blade ever cut with keener stroke than did the blade of this satirist, even when it was hidden in a madrigal or concealed in some polished sentence of prose.

As a humorist, he appreciated humor in others. When Dickens died, not another man in all the length and breadth of the land contributed so tender and beautiful a tribute to his memory as did Harte in his poem of "Dickens in Camp." The rude miners around the camp-fire drop their cards as one of them draws forth a book:

> "And then, while round them shadows gathered faster,
> And as the fire-light fell,
> He read aloud the book wherein the master
> Had writ of 'Little Nell.'
>
> "Perhaps 'twas boyish fancy—for the reader
> Was youngest of them all—
> But, as he read, from clustering pine and cedar
> A silence seemed to fall.
>
> "The fir-trees, gathering closer in the shadows,
> Listened in every spray,
> While the whole camp with 'Nell' on English meadows
> Wandered and lost their way.
>
>   *   *   *   *   *
>
> "Lost is that camp, and wasted all its fire,
> And he who wrought that spell—
> Ah! towering pine and stately Kentish spire,
> Ye have one tale to tell!

"Lost is that camp, but let its fragrant story
Blend with the breath that thrills
With hop-vines' incense all the pensive glory,
That fills the Kentish hills.

"And on that grave where English oak, and holly,
And laurel wreaths entwine,
Deem it not all a too-presumptuous folly—
This spray of western pine?"

It was left to this shy man, who came forth from the very wastes of this far-off wilderness, to lay upon the bier of the dead humorist as fragrant an offering as any mortal fellowship could suggest. It was a song in a different key—as if one having entered into the very life of the great novelist, had also for a moment entered into his death.

The wit and the poetry which ripen here are under the same sun which ripens the pomegranate and the citron. The grain and texture have always been better than that suggested by the coarser materialism without. It is little to him who is cutting his marble to the divinest form, that the whole city reeks with grime and smoke, and all its outlines are misshapen and ugly. It is little to poet or painter that sometimes the earth has only a single tint of gray, since he may also see in contrast, what a transfigured glory there may be on mountain and on sea.

There are not at any time in this dull world so many genuine humorists as one may count on his fingers. For lack of some healthy laughter the world is going to the bad. It welcomes the gentle missionary of humor, and for lack of him it often accepts those dreary counterfeits who commit assault and battery upon our mother-tongue. As in olden time the prophets were sometimes stoned in their own country, so in modern times one cannot tell whether the poet-prophet who comes up from the wilderness, will fare better or worse. Woe to him if the people cannot interpret him, or are piqued at his coming. It is a curious fact that when Harte had brought forth his first book with the modest title of *Outcroppings*, it was pelted from one end of the State to the other. It did not contain a poem of his own. But it did contain samples of the best poetry, other than his own, which had been produced in California. His critics, catching the suggestion of the title, flung at him porphyry, granite, and barren quartz, but never a rock containing a grain of gold. He might have put a torpedo into a couple of stanzas and extinguished them all. But he saw the humorous side of the assault, and enjoyed it with a keener zest than any of his assailants.

None of us would be comfortable with only some pungent sauce for dinner. But when a dreadful staleness overtakes the world, it is ready to cry out, "More sauce!" Whoever comes, therefore, bringing with him salt and seasoning, and whatever else gives a keener zest to life, never comes amiss. Sooner or later we shall know him. He will come very near to us in his books, and by that subtile law of communion which, through the brightest and noblest utterances, makes all the better world akin.

After we have seen the trick of the magician, we do not care to know him any more. But the magician of wit works by an enchantment that we can never despise. His spell is wrought with such gifts as are only given from the very heavens to here and there one. It is not the mythical Puck who is to put a girdle round the world, but the man of genius, whose thought is luminous with the light of all ages. So Shakspeare clasps the world, and Dickens belts it, and the men of wit and genius furnish each a golden thread which girds it about. The book of humor is the heart's ease. In every library it is dog-eared, because it has in it some surcease for the secret ills of life. If a million souls have been made happier for an hour through the fictions of Sir Walter Scott, what is the sum of good thus wrought? What lesser good have they wrought who have come in later times to lighten the dead weight of our overweighted lives?

Do not despise the evangel of humor because he comes unlike one of old, wearing a girdle of camel's hair, and eating his locusts and wild honey. Bear with him if he comes in flaming neck-tie and flamingo vestments, hirsute and robust. You shall know by his wit that he is no charlatan; but you cannot tell it by his raiment, nor his bill of fare. It cannot be shown that the wit of Diogenes was any better for his living in a tub. It is not probable that a dish of water-cress would inspire a better humor than a flagon of wine and a saddle of venison. I would rather look for your modern humorist in the top story of the crowded and garish hostlery; because if he is after game, he will be sure to find it there.

The exacting conditions of pioneer life are not favorable to authorship. If during this quarter of a century not a book had been written in California, we might plead in mitigation the overshadowing materialism which, while coarsely wrestling for the gains of a day, finds no place for that repose which favors culture and is fruitful of books. But over the arid plains, in the heat and dust of the long summer, one may trace the belt of green which the mountain stream carries sheer down to the sea. So there have been many thoughtful men and women who have freshened and somewhat redeemed these intellectual wastes. They have written more books in this quarter of a century than have been written in all the other States west of the Mississippi River. The publication of some of these books has cost nearly their weight in gold. During the period of twenty-five years, more than 90 volumes have been written by persons living at the time in this State.

Many of these books have had but a local circulation, and are now almost forgotten. Some have gained more than a national reputation. I enumerate among these Halleck's *International Law*; *Mountaineering*, by Clarence King; *Marine Mammals of the Northwestern Coast of North America*, by Captain Scammon; *The Luck of Roaring Camp*, by Bret Harte; and *Native Races*, by Hubert H. Bancroft. Another work just missed a more than national recognition. Grayson, the self-taught and heroic naturalist, traversed the forests and swamps of Mexico, stopping neither for morass nor jungle, until he had drawn and painted to life nearly two hundred of the rarest birds of that country. His work, which is still in sheets and manuscript, was probably at the cost of his life. But, besides the works of Audubon and Wilson, I know of nothing better in its way by any naturalist, living or dead.

No one has sought to live here exclusively by authorship. It has only been the incidental occupation of those persons who have written out of the fullness of their own lives. If they heard no mysterious voice saying unto them, "Write!" — the great mountains encamped about like sleeping dromedaries, the valleys filled with the aroma of a royal fruitage, the serene sky, and the rhythm of the great sea, all make audible signs to write. They have written out of a fresh new life.

In the streets of Herculaneum you may see the ruts made more than two thousand years ago. The grooves of society are often narrow and rigid with the fixedness of centuries. It may be better, by way of change, to propel a velocipede on a fresh track than to run four gilded wheels in the dead grooves which have been cut by the attrition of ages. After one has known the satiety which comes from the mild gabble of society, there is a wonderful freshness in a war-whoop uttered in the depths of the wilderness!

It is this large acquaintance with nature—this lying down with the mountains until one is taken into their confidence—a grim fellowship with untamed savageness—that may give a new vitality, and enlarge the horizon of intellectual life. Whence comes this man with his new poetry, which confounds the critics? and that man with his subtile wit borrowed from no school? I pray you note that for many a day his carpet hath been the *spicula* of pine, and his atmosphere hath been perfumed by the fir-tree. He has seen the mountains clad in beatific raiment of white, and their "sacristy set round with stars." He will never go so far that he will not come back to sing and talk of these, his earliest and divinest loves. So Miller sings of "The Sierra," of "Arizona," of "The Ship in the Desert." And Harte comes back again to his miner's camp, and to the larger liberty of the mountains. And there fell on Starr King a grander inspiration after he had seen the white banners of the snow-storm floating from the battlements of Yosemite.

We have brought forth nothing out of our poverty, but rather out of an affluence which could not be wholly restrained. As a gardener clips his choicest shrubs, casting the tangled riotousness of bud and blossom over the wall, so there are many here who have only trimmed a little what they have planted in their own gardens of poetry and fiction.

The little that has been done here in art is rather a sign of better things to come. Art must not only have inspiration, but it needs wealth and the society of a ripe community for its best estate. It is possible to paint for immortality in a garret. But a great deal of work done there has gone to the lumber-room. Not only must there be the fostering spirit of wealth and letters, but art also needs a picturesque world without—the grand estate of mountains and valleys, atmospheres, tones, lights, shadows—and if there be a picturesque people, we might look for a new school of art, and even famous painters. Where a poet can be inspired, there look also for the poetry which is put on canvas.

In one respect our modern civilization is nearly fatal to art. Philip Hamerton says that "a noble artist will gladly paint a peasant driving a yoke of oxen; but not a commercial traveler in his gig.... Men and women have a fatal liberty which mountains have not. They have the liberty of spoiling themselves, of making themselves ugly, and mean, and ridiculous. A mountain cannot dress in bad taste, neither is it capable of degrading itself by vice. Noble human life in a great and earnest age is better artistic material than wild nature; but human life is an age like ours is not."

If a great artist were asked to paint a fashionable woman in the prevailing stringent costume, do not blame him if he faints away. There will never get into a really great painting any of the stiff and constrained costumes of our time. Observe that the sculptor rarely cuts the statute of a modern statesman without the accessories of some flowing and graceful attire. He cannot sculpture a modern dress-suit without feeling that he has offered an affront to art.

But in spite of our civilization there is a great deal that is picturesque among the people—the Parsee, Mohammedan, Malay, and Mongol, whom one may sometimes meet on the same street—the red shirt of the Italian fisherman, and the lateen sail which sends his boat flying over the water. The very distresses and distraits of men here have made them picturesque. I have seen a valedictorian of a leading college deep down in a gravel mine, directing his hydraulic pipe against the bank. Clad in a gray shirt and slouch-hat, he was a far better subject for a painter than on the day he took his degree. The native Californian on horseback, with *poncho*, *sombrero*, and leggings, is a good subject for the canvas, as well as the quaint old church where he worships, so rich in its very ruins. Moreover, the whole physical aspect of the country is wonderfully picturesque. The palm tree lifting up its fronded head in the desert, the great fir tree set against the ineffable azure of the heavens, the vine-clad hills, the serrated mountains which the frosts have canonized with their sealed and unsealed fountains, and all the gold and purple which touch the hills at even-tide—these are the rich ministries of nature. It may take art a thousand years to ripen even here. For how many years had the long procession of painters come and gone before Raphael and Michael Angelo appeared?

Our young art school will some day have its treasures; and there will be hung on these walls the portraits of other men whose culture and influence will be worth more than all the gold of the mountains. Let the artist set up his easel and write his silent poem upon the canvas. Welcome all influences which soften this hard and barren materialism. Before the mountains were unvexed by the miner's drill the land itself was a poem and a picture. One day the turbid streams will turn to crystal again, and the only miner will be the living glacier sitting on its white throne of judgment and grinding the very mountains to powder. Fortunate they who can catch this wealth of inspiration. These are the ministers and prophets whose larger and finer interpretation of nature are part of the treasures of the new commonwealth.

Lector House believes that a society develops through a two-fold approach of continuous learning and adaptation, which is derived from the study of classic literary works spread across the historic timeline of literature records. Therefore, we aim at reviving, repairing and redeveloping all those inaccessible or damaged but historically as well as culturally important literature across subjects so that the future generations may have an opportunity to study and learn from past works to embark upon a journey of creating a better future.

This book is a result of an effort made by Lector House towards making a contribution to the preservation and repair of original ancient works which might hold historical significance to the approach of continuous learning across subjects.

HAPPY READING & LEARNING!

LECTOR HOUSE LLP
E-MAIL: lectorpublishing@gmail.com

Lector House believes that a society develops through a two-fold approach of continuous learning and adaptation, which is derived from the study of classic literary works spread across the historic timeline of literature records. Therefore, we aim at reviving, repairing and redeveloping all those inaccessible or damaged but historically as well as culturally important literature across subjects so that the future generations may have an opportunity to study and learn from past works to embark upon a journey of creating a better future.

This book is a result of an effort made by Lector House towards making a contribution to the preservation and repair of original ancient works which might hold historical significance to the approach of continuous learning across subjects.

HAPPY READING & LEARNING!

LECTOR HOUSE LLP
E-MAIL: lectorpublishing@gmail.com